RED GOLDFISH

PROMO EDITION

HOW PROMOTIONAL PRODUCTS LEVERAGE
PURPOSE TO INCREASE IMPACT

Stan Phelps & Roger Burnett

Red Goldfish Promo Edition

© 2020 by Stan Phelps and Roger Burnett

Published by 9 INCH marketing

Copy Editing by Lee Heinrich of Write Way Publishing
Cover by Josh Vaughan and Layout by Amit Dey

ISBN: 978-1-952234-09-5

1. Purpose 2. Leadership 3. Culture 4. Promotional Products

First Printing: 2020

Printed in the United States of America

Red Goldfish Promo Edition is available for bulk orders. For further details and special pricing, please email stan@purplegoldfish.com.

DEDICATION

This book is dedicated to my good friend Danny Rosin. He is a pioneer in showing how a promotional product can embody purpose and create a meaningful experience.

— Stan Phelps

This book is dedicated to my wife Melisa, for without her there is not a book.

— Roger Burnett

ACKNOWLEDGMENTS

We'd like to thank everyone who inspired us, supported us, or provided feedback for the book:

Sean Annable, Paul Bellantone, Melinda Bowden, Rod Brown, John Bruellman, Melisa Burnett, Evan Carroll, Kathy Cheng, Kellie Claudio, Karie Cowden, Brittany David, Ray DelMuro, Amit Dey, Stan Dohan, Dan Edge, Robert Fiveash, Kevin Flynn, Charity Gibson, Lynn Glover, Mark and Britney Godsey, Bill Grassmyer, Jim Hagan, Kirby Hasseman, Lee Heinrich, Peter Hirsch, Dena Hirschberg, Tim Howe, Jonathan Irvin, Kara Keister, Paul Kiewiet, Deb and Barry Lipsett, Jeremy Lott, Rob Lowe, Brandon Mackay, Dan Nevins, Bill Petrie, Jennifer Phelps, Devin Piscitelli, Tony Poston, Jeremy Priest, Nate Robson, Danny Rosin, Leeatt Rothschild, Mandi Rudd, Jodie Schillinger, David Shultz, Denise Taschereau, Joshua Vaughan, Tony Wavering, and Brian Young.

FOREWORD

"Try to do good in the world, not out of fear from hell or reward from heaven, but because it feels better not to be an asshole."

—Danny Rosin

It is my privilege to share my support of *Red Goldfish Promo Edition* because, first, I am close friends with the authors and second, I have witnessed their altruism and commitment to selling with purpose. They are good humans who have inspired me to be a better employer, parent, husband, and champion of nonprofits.

Sure, Roger and Stan deliver all the stats and feels you need to giddy-up as a purpose-driven business with a little more soul.

Yet, I would say that *Red Goldfish Promo Edition* is for you if you:

- Want to build a brand that moves at the speed of trust.

- Are a small fish (these guys love fish references) in a big pond but are looking for differentiation with purpose as your calling card.

- Agree that marketing is about showing, not telling through cute jingles.

- Are looking for a role in cause-marketing.

- Hope to transform job satisfaction and ethical leadership.

Now is the time to align your brand with more purpose to attract loyal talent and clients and ultimately, build a stronger valuation. Your staff, customers, community, and Momma Earth are betting on you right now.

I believe that digital spaces are crowded, consumers find gratification in ad-blocking, and the internet has dehumanized businesses. I also love a thoughtful and creative gift. It's one reason I have been loyal to a promotional marketing career for 30 years. And in this book, you will discover that a physical branded giveaway can also be connected to supporting nonprofits, sustainable initiatives, and give people a stronger emotional connection to your brand. This is what our industry calls "The #PowerofPromo."

Yet, all of this begs many questions. What will you do to make *purpose* your ultimate differentiator? Will your brand take a stand for something? Will it make a positive difference in your community? Will customers and employees use the word "love" when they talk about your organization? Will you rewrite your brand's mission? How can you further humanize your business? And how might promotional products help you tell a compelling story to enhance your brand's reputation?

As you "wrassle" with these business-defining questions, *Red Goldfish Promo Edition* will give you evidence and advice as well as lay out a plan that includes more purpose as well as profit. If nothing else, it will open your eyes and heart. The world needs more of that right now.

— DANNY ROSIN

Danny Rosin is the Co-Founder of Brand Fuel, Band Together, PromoCares, PromoKitchen, Reciprocity Road, and Operation Smile's youth groups. Danny serves on the boards of Promotional Products Assoc. International, American Marketing Association (Triangle Chapter), A Place at The Table, and Arc Benders.

TABLE OF CONTENTS

INTRODUCTION

BY ROGER BURNETT

"(Strategy x Execution) x Trust = Results"

– Stephen M.R. Covey

"Why are we lying on the floor?"

Such began a conversation that would forever shape my life and have a major impact on the way I approached work in what is now a 25-year professional sales career, and the first of what would be two separate times when lying on that same floor changed the trajectory of my life.

*"There's a **salesperson** at the door . . ." (she said to me through clenched teeth.)*

The 7-year-old me was curious and undeterred by this sudden change in condition. Many "persons" crossed our threshold in an average week, and in zero percent of those other situations had I ever been ordered to the floor. What was the significance of the term "salesperson" that created this need for stealthiness?

What Mom proceeded to say at that moment shaped my entire life. In my mom's world as a young woman, the presence of a sales-person was met with cynicism, skepticism, and a healthy dose of near-violent disdain. Had one of the men of the family been home, the assuredly fine gentleman on the other side of the door would have had a far more difficult problem on his hands than the lady of the house and her son pretending not to be home. It was the result of tactics, strategies, and downright dirty tricks at the hands of other traveling salespeople that had ruined the possibility of a more civilized door-to-door version of commerce in our neighborhood. There were daily and weekly interactions with the mailman, the paper delivery person, the milkman, the street sweeper, the trash collectors, the diaper delivery service, and more, depending on your dad's class rank in the unions protecting American manufacturing workers. We were used to hanging around with other *people*, so it was especially clear to me just how disdainfully door-to-door salespeople as a general class of society were viewed, an attitude I won't ever be able to shake.

Imagine my surprise when the young adult version of me repeatedly heard the same suggestion—

*"Roger, you would make a **terrific** salesperson!" (sad face, confused face, shaking my head)*

Unknowingly, at the moment on the floor as we hid from that salesperson, my mom created for me a source of internal conflict that haunted me in varying stages of my sales career. By the time I was in my teens, I could see in myself the personality traits that suggested others were right on the mark in their predictions of sales aptitude, but it was a recurring source of conflict as I navigated the early stages of my professional sales career.

It didn't take long before the competitor in me struggled with that conflict. I saw people around me achieving success without the problems between their ears I was dealing with, and it was in that moment of watching others achieve the success I longed for that I reconciled once and for all that I was going to have to learn how to win the day and defeat my inner conflict. The choice I made changed the course of my career and has lived with me to this day.

At that moment, I made a conscious choice to become **The Anti-Salesperson**. This was the era of selling before the internet, where often the buyer of that which you sold not only had a poor understanding of the financials of a basic transaction but also had precious little access to information that might assist in evaluating potential options. Such was sales prior to the internet, and to many salespeople, selling held a healthy dose of the Latin phrase *caveat emptor* or *the principle that the buyer alone is responsible for checking the quality and suitability of goods before a purchase is made*. Without the power of the internet, the real power in the transaction lay in the buyer's ability to learn the best questions to ask of sellers—no easy feat for complicated pieces of equipment like copy machines, cars, word processors, typewriters, and even calculators (the very first handheld computers).

As *The Anti-Salesperson*, I assumed the role of educator, arming potential buyers with the information necessary to make the best possible decision when choosing between seemingly similar options. To win using this strategy, I needed to be a good questioner with the goal to help each buyer determine the questions to ask to make the best buying decision. And I needed to be sufficiently credible to arm the prospect with whatever questions I thought they were going to need to make a good choice based on the approach they were using. On top of that, most people were pretty used to getting screwed over by the average salesperson, so it was important to make people understand just how often I heard how other people around town were taking advantage of folks. Think of me as a walking Yelp! Review for my era. I wanted it to be abundantly clear that I was not interested in sharing information that wasn't true, but I would offer an opinion based on facts and accumulated stories of interactions with others in my day-to-day sales activities if asked.

By assuming the persona of *The Anti-Salesperson*, I transformed my conflict away from feeling like I was the guy on the porch my mom would still hide from even today to the guy who was giving power back to the people.

Did I always win? NO

Did I win my fair share? Unequivocally, YES! (Especially with a very specific demographic that only years later did I come to understand.)

Did I learn how to equip buyers with the questions my competition didn't want to be asked? WELL . . .

Not at first, but as my understanding of the strategy grew, so did my ability to uncover truths previously hidden by most salespeople, and in return, our success rate followed.

By finding a way to reconcile the conflict I felt with an altruistic attempt to turn the game in favor *of the buyer*, I was able to achieve superstar sales success and go on to direct the efforts of some of the highest performing teams in the spaces in which we sold.

A LITTLE SOMETHING EXTRA

My devotion to the concept of differentiation via added value is rooted in the pre-internet era of selling, and yet, with the advent of the web and the power it has given the buyer, nothing has changed. It is still up to the seller to prove to buyers that what they sell IS the best option—that their service or product best equips the buyer on THEIR journey. So, be the guide. Show the way. Surprise and delight are the order of the day. What I've come to learn in my years in sales is the immense value in the concept that Stan Phelps helped me identify by name—lagniappe, doing something just a little extra and unexpected, one of the most beloved contributions to society, originating from the creole culture that calls New Orleans home.

How could I refashion this *Anti-Salesperson* persona for the internet era? Like a forgotten superhero, my powers were rendered temporarily useless by a nameless, faceless enemy called the World Wide Web. How might I inject added value to an otherwise potentially frictionless transaction executed without ANY human interaction, fueled by the instantaneous answers available via internet research?

As my approach evolved away from being a reliable source of questions, I considered how the need for expertise would change in the era of abundant information. It was in that self-analysis that I realized there were new ways the need for trust was manifesting in an online world. Consumers rely on and form opinions of brands as informed by a healthy dose of personal participation in and use of peer review platforms (Airbnb, Uber, etc.). On these crowdsourced, consumer driven platforms, your reputation and corresponding reviews supporting your reputation give you the ability to earn a tiered set of rewards for successful behavior modification. (My wife and I are Airbnb SuperHosts, and we're proud of that status!) I've made it my mission to study and recognize how to display expertise and character in the places where buyers go to learn and develop a new strategy that takes advantage of the inherent opportunities to be seen as an expert online.

Sales-driven organizations who have not yet evolved away from a sales-training strategy that focuses primarily on product knowledge are in peril. Many sales leaders recognize the failures their training strategy creates but have been unwilling, underfunded, or not sure what to do as a replacement, and a 10-year uninterrupted run of economic prosperity covered up a lot of short-comings on the part of many a sales organization.

To succeed in the post COVID-19 economy, salespeople must be allowed to marry their personalities, beliefs, and those individual characteristics that would make them likeable to prospective buyers in combination with strong knowledge of their products and/

or services. This requires a dedicated effort on the part of every company to evolve their training programs to meet this new, human-centered strategy, where your staff members are a part of your brand.

Regardless of vocation, each of us needs to formulate and internalize a strategy to be able to document and broadcast our individual areas of interest, knowledge, and ultimately, expertise. It's no longer sufficient to merely be good at what we do. You can't get away with not knowing your product, but prospects will be more willing to give you the benefit of the doubt if they've had an opportunity to get immersed in your brand in this way—by showing the personalities behind your operation, you shorten the path to creating connection with buyers and increase empathy for your brand.

In this work era, your personal marketability needs to be on display in a manner consistent with who you are, and it also must be shareable and findable in those instances where you'd want the opportunity to display your interests, knowledge, and expertise. It's time to migrate your contributions to Reddit Boards to a broader cross-section of places where more eyes can see your work. It's time for the long-form social media posts you make about your passions to become a page on Medium.

If you want the best work, you have to be seen as an expert, and without the opportunity for those seeking your expertise to learn about what you know best, you're introducing an element of added calorie consumption in the minds of consumers to decide if you're a worthy choice. Failing to adopt a broadcast strategy won't always get you left out of consideration, but it does create the opportunity to cost you chances when others are putting out that kind of work and you're not.

This book covers in detail an argument for purpose as a means of creating differentiation via added value. In this instance, the added value is found in the direct benefits and the corresponding ripple effects that happen when for-profit businesses adopt values consistent with making the lives of the people in contact with their brand better. Avenues to seek your purpose range from employees to the community you live and work in to the environment.

In my years of research investigating purpose as a business strategy, I've reported stories of record sales, improved profits, more productive employees, and better relationships with suppliers. The stories were so dramatically compelling that I was inspired to open my own business and adopt a purpose-focused mission married with a for-profit vision. The results were so gratifying that I opened a second new business built on the same principles in a completely different marketplace the following year. While the workload is significant, the load is lightened by the proximity of the work to my personal why, and the ways that we do what we as a company in our industry do is perfectly aligned with who we are as people.

The Anti-Salesperson is alive and well, bringing added value by using what we do to make the world a better place and by aligning with other businesses and consumers interested in doing the same thing. I'm not alone. The stories in this book are a reflection of more than 250 examples of the different ways businesses in the Promotional Marketing industry are spreading goodness into the world. Here's hoping you too get a sense of inspiration as you read along. Should you feel compelled to action as I was, the second half of the book uncovers some great ways you can get started on your own road to purpose.

PREFACE

PURPOSE BY THE NUMBERS

10 Statistics That Make the Case for Purpose in Promotional Products

10. In *Firms of Endearment*, Raj Sisodia looked at 28 companies based on characteristics such as their stated purpose, generosity of compensation, quality of customer service, investment in their communities, and impact on the environment. He found that 18 publicly traded companies out of the 28 outperformed the S&P 500 index by a factor of 10.5 over the years 1996-2011. Source: HBR[1]

9. 90 percent of executives surveyed said their company understands the importance of purpose, but only 46 percent said it informs their strategic and operational decision-making. Source: EY[2]

8. According to Brand Fuel, all things being equal, 86 percent of customers will choose to do business with companies whose values mesh with their own.

7. 81 percent of manufacturers and 73 percent of retailers acknowledge that environmental and social impact programs are a way to reduce risk. Source: Ketchum-CCOP[3]

---

1. https://hbr.org/2013/04/companies-that-practice-conscious-capitalism-perform
2. http://www.ey.com/Publication/vwLUAssets/ey-the-business-case-for-purpose/$FILE/ey-the-business-case-for-purpose.pdf
3. http://www.sustainablebrands.com/news_and_views/stakeholder_trends_insights/hannah_furlong/
competitiveness_reputation_deliver_higher_ROI

6. 6 out of 7 employees would consider leaving an employer whose values no longer meet their expectations. Source: PriceWaterhouseCoopers[4]

5. 58 percent of companies with a clearly articulated and understood purpose experienced growth of +10%. Source: 2016 Global Purpose Index[5]

4. Companies that embrace purpose have a 44 percent higher employee retention rate. Source: Gallup

3. Purpose increases sales by 37 percent. Source: Shawn Achor

2. Purposeful, value-driven companies outperform their counterparts by a factor of 12. Source: *Corporate Culture & Performance*, by John Kotter and James Heskett[6]

1. Capitalism may have the ability to end poverty on Earth. The percentage of people living on less than $1 per day has dropped from 85 percent in 1820 to 17 percent in 2003. If current trends continue, poverty will be virtually eliminated in the next 50 years. Source: World Bank[7]

4. https://www.pwc.com/m1/en/services/consulting/documents/millennials-at-work.pdf

5. https://cdn.imperative.com/media/public/Global_Purpose_Index_2016.pdf

6. https://www.amazon.com/Corporate-Culture-Performance-John-Kotter/dp/1451655320

7. http://www.sandermahieu.com/wp-content/uploads/2015/03/Raj-Sisodia-Conscious-Capitalism-Presentation-BVC-South-Africa.pdf

SECTION I:

WHAT IS A RED GOLDFISH? (THE WHY)

CHAPTER 1

THE CASE FOR PURPOSE IN PROMO

*"Consumers want a better world,
not just better widgets."*

– Simon Mainwaring

W hile it's been some time since the Promotional Marketing (Promo) industry crossed into its maturity phase, our growth as a marketplace has outpaced GDP. We closely mirrored GDP in 2015 (3.8% v. 2.9% GDP) and 2016 (2.4% v. 1.6%) only to witness a period of explosive outperformance in 2017 (9.3% v. 2.4%) and 2018 (6.3% v. 2.9%) (PPAI Research) Promotional marketing has also outpaced sales performance by other advertising media in the same period.

Promotional marketing is an effective and relatively inexpensive medium capable of delivering a sensory experience that appeals to late-stage Millennials and to Gen Zers. They've grown up in an age of financial stability that afforded them the chance to explore unlike any generation before them. Theirs is the Instagram generation of documenters of all things celebratory—their way of recording the world is from their personal purview, in the immediate moment—with an array of amazing technological tools at their fingertips. My children (all in their 20s) have a mutually held belief that today, **right now,** is the most incredible time in the evolution of the world to be alive. Not only do they want to go on adventures, they also want to have things that remind them of the adventure. Along with the Instagram posts, they want a cool hat, a pair of interesting sunglasses, or some other small reminder of the time spent, and those things usually end up making their way into the posts.

For many Millennials and Gen Zers, branding extends beyond what traditionally has been the relationship between marketers and consumers. Since this wide age group has been documenting their personal journeys since they were very young, the result is individuals who perceive *themselves* to be a brand—a notion only reinforced by the emergence of paid social media influencers. They conduct their activities on social media in the same curated, made-for-sponsorship way that their heroes who are getting paid are doing.

As a result, decisions made about the type and brand of clothes worn in social media posts can become part of the story behind the account holder's personal brand. If your brand's values don't align with the image this demographic is attempting to portray in the building of their *own* brand, you're not making the cut, no matter what marketing money you throw at them.

This notion of branding as personal ideology was never as central to the public discourse as it was when Nike introduced the Colin Kaepernick campaign. Nike's *"Believe in something. Even if it means sacrificing everything."* campaign was timed to mark the start of the 2018/19 NFL season and was intended to celebrate the 30th anniversary of the launch of Nike's famous Just Do It tagline. Kaepernick was a flashpoint character for his personal protest against police brutality and then his subsequent legal battle with the league regarding his allegations of team collusion against him, as he has never been approached to play for any other team since kneeling for the national anthem prior to San Francisco 49er football games during the 2016 season.

Nike's decision to publicly support the still unemployed and frequently derided former quarterback represented an inflection point for consumers as they considered their opinion of the brand in light of Nike's support for Kaepernick. In a *Fast Company* interview[8] about his choice to approve the ad, Nike founder Phil Knight had this to offer with respect to his decision-making:

> "It doesn't matter how many people hate your brand as long as enough people love it. And as long as you have that attitude, you can't be afraid of offending people. You can't try and go down the middle of the road. You have to take a stand on something, which is ultimately I think why the Kaepernick ad worked."

With the release of the Kaepernick campaign, it immediately thrust the brand front and center in the ideological scales of almost every consumer. We were suddenly forced into deciding whether or not the choice Nike had made was consistent with our own values and what our personal reaction needed to be in light of this new information. It was uncomfortable for many. The responses spanned the gamut from the requisite burning of Nike products in the street to Nike realizing $163 million in earned media, a $6 billion brand value increase, and a 31 percent boost in sales.

Nike has a long history of taking controversial stands in their advertising, but in the post-Jordan era, Nike the brand had taken a more comfortable approach to its marketing, offering more aspirational and outcome-based messages designed to fuel our desire

8. https://www.fastcompany.com/90314699/nike-cofounder-why-i-approved-the-controversial-colin-kaepernick-ad

to achieve new personal bests, not necessarily shaking up society in the process. As a result, many of us welcomed Nike into our most-trusted brands' line-up, assuming greater levels of comfort with the consistency the brand provided. This happened regardless of what may have been happening at the Company over the years, including child labor violations and sexual harassment threats that led to a mass exodus of male employees.

As you consider your own purchases, spend some time thinking about the brands you make a regular part of your life. The car you drive. The coffee you drink. Your favorite clothing line. The sports teams you root for. Each of these choices reinforces a narrative you've built for yourself, and, for many, the brands with which you surround yourself are an outward expression of your ideology. By choosing to create and ultimately release the Kaepernick campaign, Nike was taking a calculated risk that the attitudes and belief system of younger buyers would align with supporting Kaepernick. They couched the ad in the concept of fighting for something bigger than oneself—a lesson well-learned by the inclusive and activist-natured Generation Z.

If you've not done so before, spend some time taking a personal inventory of the brands and products you most frequently buy. Do the companies selling those products have values that align with your own? It can be eye-opening when you take the time to consider how the money you spend in your own household may be supporting outcomes you wouldn't otherwise be proud to support with firsthand knowledge.

The same often holds true for those responsible for putting their company brand on promotional marketing items. Even though our medium has proven time and again it achieves measurable results when used thoughtfully and strategically and even though there are ad-agency-level promotional marketing organizations in many local communities capable of delivering exceptional value, branded merchandise is often an after-thought for the average company. Promotional products are sometimes seen as a nuisance purchase and often driven by searches for lowest cost products, frequently executed with no interaction with a specialist in the field, more and more frequently executed via e-commerce providers who've stepped in to provide the most Amazon-like experience possible for buyers seeking these frictionless transactions.

As of 2018, web sales comprised 24 percent of all purchases of promotional marketing items, a statistic that is sure to report higher when numbers are available in coming years. Additionally, an influx of venture capital has accelerated a growing consolidation of players on both the Distributor and Supplier side of the supply chain. While the industry is large, there has been no dominant player, no single source for product capable of single-handedly dictating to its supply chain the way commerce would be transacted in the style of Walmart's take it or leave it proposition with their suppliers.

With many $50MM+ acquisitions in the last 2 years and previously held beliefs crumbling in the face of a post-COVID-19 economy, there will be even greater consolidation coming. All members of this complicated and multi-part supply chain will have to consider the merit of each other as partners going forward. The rules that applied prior to the pandemic may need to be changed to ensure a successful future for our industry.

In an industry populated with an aging base of salespeople and filled with those who view the sale of promotional products as side-gigs and add-ons to other lines of business, it's possible we will see an accelerated contraction of suppliers given the pressures of staying in business when there appears to be no business to be had. For those companies that remain, the ability to provide additional value beyond the sale of product will be of unprecedented necessity. The concepts and principles of lagniappe and Stan's work with The Goldfish Project will never have been more important. Once we're able to assess the new landscape and get a look at the way things have changed, each of us, regardless of departmental role or spot on the organizational chart, will have to re-learn how to be of value.

I had the good fortune to hear a presentation made by one of the most informed members of our marketplace, David Nicholson of Polyconcept North America. In the presentation, David examined the ways the promotional products marketplace is following a similar path to what has happened in the pizza industry. Absent any real opportunity for differentiation (pizza is pizza) and relative inelasticity of growth in new ideas in pizza (stuffed crust, anyone?), the only way to compete is with technology.

This is where the divide is starting to create separation in pizza chains. Mom and Pops don't have the money to invest in technology, so they are being slowly forced out by the pizza chains that have the resources to invest in ways to better communicate with their customers. Apparently everyone wants to know what's going on with their pizza. Domino's occupies the top spot in the pizza wars largely because of 1-click ordering, even while accepting that their product is inferior to their competitors.

The same is happening in the Promotional Marketing industry as the larger companies in the marketplace continue to make heavy investments in technology in an effort to level the playing field with prospective marketplace threats like Amazon and Walmart.

If you're a small fish in this (or any) pond, it will become essential for you to be able to communicate what it is about what you do that would make people want to give you their money. If you can't tell the average person what it is that would make them change how they already do things, especially in these emotional and chaotic times, the likelihood of a change occurring is virtually nil. Buyers of promotional marketing items have numerous and relatively simple options to render your value completely useless, so it's imperative you create something to give yourself a chance to be seen as their best option.

Given this obstacle, what might you do to approach this challenge?

There are a number of approaches you might take to establish credibility and authority as a best option. For example, feature Made in the USA products, offer a specific needed product like hand sanitizer with company logos, or address a vertical market where you source for everything branded for healthcare companies.

Each of these is an attempt to create an opportunity for alignment. If the buyer at your prospect company is the child of a line worker who lost a job to Mexico or China, that buyer might be a little more amenable to Made in the USA products than in years past. If the COVID-19 experience ensures anything, it is that hand sanitizer will become the new reusable water bottle. If you understand how to support an overwhelmed industry like healthcare in a time of crisis, your services will prove to be invaluable.

In times of scarce resources, human beings have an inherent need to feel as though we are making good decisions, and such decisions are usually built on a foundation of trust. Without this trust, the velocity of change slows to a near halt. Alignment opportunities present a chance for buyers to see you as an authority and, moreover, a helpful partner.

Which brings us to purpose.

Our historical nature has been an industry willing to write an order with no consideration for what the sum effect of that transaction might have on the environment and the world. We have sold and do sell shit that is BRANDFILL—merely poorly executed, cheap, non-useful products sourced and logoed that do nothing more than check a box on the to-do list of the buyer. Brandfill is embarrassing and harmful to the buyer, the seller, and the environment. This has created some heaviness within our peer group.

On the other side of the token, we've witnessed/been the creators and producers of/collaborated on things that were 180 degrees opposite of the way our medium had historically (and truthfully) been marginalized. We've witnessed instances where the use of our medium created an opportunity to extend a memory beyond the moment and commemorated a time in life worthy of remembrance. We've seen the ways our creative minds solved problems for businesses of all kinds and the ways our medium elevated itself to the heights of marketing.

What we have witnessed with organizations seeking a competitive differentiator is that those choosing purpose as the North Star of their methodology have created impressive results as a group. A 2015 study by Havas Worldwide found that brands that ranked high on purpose and meaning experienced as much as 46 percent more market success than lower-rated brands. An Insights 2020 study sponsored by the Advertising Research Foundation found that 86 percent of companies that over-perform on revenue growth linked everything they do to purpose. In the book *Grow* by Jim Collins, research partner Millward-Brown Optimor found that the Stengel 50 of purpose-driven companies experienced 10 years of pace-setting growth. Research from Deloitte Insights suggests companies aligned on purpose report 30 percent higher levels of innovation and 40 percent higher levels of workforce retention than competitors.

Emerging demographics for promotional product buyers have demonstrated a strong desire for authenticity and transparency from companies whose products or services they buy. They want to know what's going on with their money, beyond receiving the product/service, when they give it to that supplier. The more they care, the harder they'll dig, and the more they'll use that as their key decision-making criterion, be it in their personal lives or in the roles they are starting to assume in corporate America. This desire for transparency also drives decision-making for many on where they want to work.

Purpose is universal. People 20 to 60 years old ALL self-identify with the idea that something bigger than themselves was a key decision-making criteria when determining their relationship with their employer. Consider the following February 2018 *Harvard Business Review* article, where evaluators determined the three largest contributing factors for employee engagement, regardless of age demographic:

1. Career: provides autonomy, enhances strengths, and promotes development

2. Community: fosters a sense of connection, respect, and being cared about and recognized by others

3. Cause: offers the opportunity to make an impact through identifying with the organizational mission and believing that it does good in the world

If you consider the way purpose offers a unique opportunity to build an emotional relationship with your customers, imagine the transformative nature of the way promotional marketing items might become sought-after extensions of your brand. Your customers will no longer be merely purchasers of what you sell, they'll become advocates for your brand. Ask Yeti. See Harley Davidson. Your business has the same opportunity to become a sought-after product if you execute well, and emerging buyer demographics are hungry for the chance to connect this way.

While many avenues for alignment are effective, purpose has the broadest reach and has the best chance to be a generational unifier.

Alignment is one of the fastest-growing challenges in the face of COVID-19 attacks from both sides of the Boomer-Millennial generational conflict. Aligning purpose is by an order of magnitude more appealing because it is more appealing to a wider audience than other choices.

But don't take our word for it. This book is loaded with case studies, examples, and profiles of companies of all sizes, from all 3 sides of our supply chain (Suppliers, Distributors, and Service Providers). From the research gathered for this book, we identified themes to examine as you consider the potential for alignment on purpose for your own business. Plus, you'll encounter profiles of organizations just like yours showcasing their own alignment efforts.

Before we dive into the specifics of the Promotional Marketing industry and the amazing purpose-driven people you'll discover, let's first consider some of the finer points behind the growth of popularity in aligning on purpose as a business strategy and look at some of the guideposts that were created along the way.

CHAPTER 2

PURPOSE IS THE NEW BLACK

*"Corporate purpose is at the confluence of
strategy and values.
It expresses the company's fundamental - the raison
d'être or overriding reason for existing. It is the end to
which the strategy is directed."*

– Richard Ellsworth

Purpose is becoming the new black. It is emerging as a guiding light that can help business navigate and thrive in the 21st century. According to the EY Pursuit of Purpose Study, "Purpose—an aspirational reason for being that is grounded in humanity—is at the core of how many companies are responding to the business and societal challenges of today."

What can happen if you put purpose at the core of your business? Here are 10 benefits from the EY Purpose Study:[9]

1. Purpose instills strategic clarity.

2. Purpose guides both short-term decisions and long-term strategy at every level of an organization, encouraging leaders to think about systems holistically.

3. Purpose guides choices about what not to do as well as what to do.

4. Purpose channels innovation.

5. Purpose is a force for and a response to transformation.

6. Purpose motivates people through meaning, not fear. It clarifies the long-term outcome so people understand the need for change rather than feeling it is imposed upon them.

7. Purpose is also a response to societal pressures on business to transform, to address global challenges, and to take a longer-term, more comprehensive approach for growth and value.

8. Purpose taps a universal need to contribute, to feel a part of society.

9. Purpose recognizes differences and diversity. Purpose builds bridges.

10. Purpose helps individuals/teams work across silos to pursue a single, compelling aim.

---

9. http://www.ey.com/Publication/vwLUAssets/EY-pursuit-of-purpose-exec-sum/$FILE/EY-pursuit-of-purpose-exec-sum.pdf

WIN-WIN-WIN

Organizations that have a defined purpose benefit from a win-win-win scenario. By standing for something bigger than just their products/services, organizations are winning on three levels:

Win #1: Employees – Purpose helps attract the best talent, keeps them engaged, and retains them. Purpose is important to employees. It helps determine the values of an organization.

Win #2: Customers – Purpose becomes a differentiator that drives acquisition and retention. It also helps the business stay competitive. It provides a reason for their customers to engage. Purpose is important to customers as it showcases the values of an organization. According to Brand Fuel, "All things being equal, 6 out of 7 customers will choose to do business with companies whose values mesh with their own."

Win #3: Shareholders - Purpose has positive effects on key performance drivers. Research shows that companies who clearly articulate their purpose enjoy higher growth rates than competitors who do not.

The Difference Between a Mission Statement and Purpose Statement

It is important to differentiate between an organization's mission and its purpose.

Mission: To define its mission, a company should answer some basic questions. According to Peter Drucker, a mission statement would answer, "What is our business? Who is the customer? What is of value to the customer? What will our business be? What should our business be?"[10] It aims to stand for the "what" and "who" to help guide the business.

---

10. http://marketinginfoz.blogspot.com/2013/10/defining-corporate-mission.html

Purpose: To define corporate purpose, a company begins with its reason for being, its *raison d'être*. It's the fundamental "why" the company was first started. A purpose statement not only references the "who," it goes deeper to uncover the aspirational needs of its customers. David Packard, co-founder of Hewlett-Packard, shared his thoughts on purpose with a training group in 1960:[11]

> I want to discuss why a company exists in the first place. In other words, why are we here? I think many people assume, wrongly, that a company exists simply to make money. While this is an important result of a company's existence, we have to go deeper and find the real reasons for our being. . . . Purpose (which should last at least 100 years) should not be confused with specific goals or business strategies (which should change many times in 100 years). Whereas you might achieve a goal or complete a strategy, you cannot fulfill a purpose; it's like a guiding star on the horizon—forever pursued but never reached. Yet although purpose itself does not change, it does inspire change. The very fact that purpose can never be fully realized means that an organization can never stop stimulating change and progress.

> The table on the next page shows the difference between mission and purpose.

11. https://disneyinstitute.com/blog/2015/04/mission-versus-purpose-whats-the-difference/346/

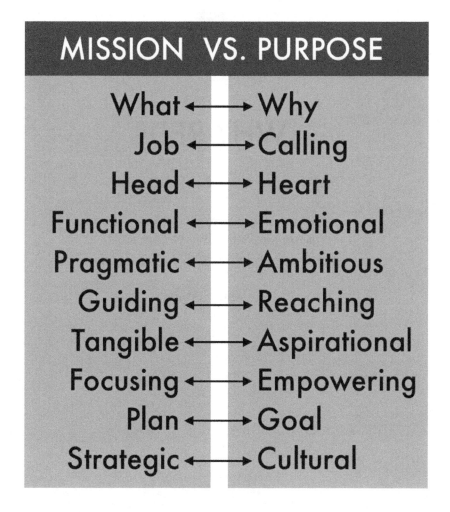

MISSION VS. PURPOSE

What	Why
Job	Calling
Head	Heart
Functional	Emotional
Pragmatic	Ambitious
Guiding	Reaching
Tangible	Aspirational
Focusing	Empowering
Plan	Goal
Strategic	Cultural

BRINGING PURPOSE TO LIFE

According to Gallup, when it comes to communicating an organization's purpose to employees, customers, and stakeholders, words don't matter nearly as much as actions do. Companies need to find ways to bring purpose to life. Creating little things that can make a big difference for employees, customers, and society is one way. Red Goldfish are the little things you do to bring purpose to life. The next two chapters will explain the meaning behind a Red Goldfish. Specifically, why red and why a goldfish.

CHAPTER 3

WHY RED?

"We picked up one excellent word—a word
worth traveling to New Orleans to get;
a nice limber, expressive, handy word—lagniappe"

- Mark Twain

Red is the fifth color in the Goldfish series of books. The initial colored trilogy of books was an ode to an iconic American city and its most famous event. That city is New Orleans. Purple, green, and gold are the three official colors of Mardi Gras. It's a reference to New Orleans because there is one word from New Orleans that exemplifies the concept of doing a little something extra. That word is lagniappe. Pronounced *lan-yap*, it is a creole word for an "added gift" or "to give more." The practice originated in Louisiana in the 1840s whereby a merchant would give a customer a little something extra at the time of purchase. It is a signature personal touch by the business that creates goodwill and promotes word of mouth.

According to Webster's:[12]

> **LAGNIAPPE** (lanˈyəəp, lăn-yăpˈ) *Chiefly Southern Louisiana & Mississippi*

1. A small gift presented by a store owner to a customer with the customer's purchase.

2. An extra or unexpected gift or benefit. Also called *boot.*

Mark Twain was smitten with the word. He wrote about lagniappe in his autobiography, *Life on the Mississippi*:

> We picked up one excellent word—a word worth traveling to New Orleans to get; a nice limber, expressive, handy word—"lagniappe." They pronounce it lanny-yap. It is Spanish—so they said. We discovered it at the head of a column of odds and ends in the [Times] Picayune [newspaper] the first day; heard twenty people use it the second; inquired what it meant the third; adopted it and got facility in swinging it the fourth. It

---

12. https://www.merriam-webster.com/dictionary/lagniappe

has a restricted meaning, but I think the people spread it out a little when they choose. It is the equivalent of the thirteenth roll in a baker's dozen. It is something thrown in, gratis, for good measure.

In the trilogy, *Purple Goldfish* focused on the little things you could do to improve the customer experience, *Green Goldfish* (co-authored with Lauren McGhee) examined how to drive engagement to improve the employee experience, and *Golden Goldfish* uncovered the importance of taking care of your best customers/employees.

The fourth book, *Blue Goldfish* (co-authored with Evan Carroll), revealed how to leverage technology, data, and analytics to improve the customer experience. Blue was a reference to a 10th-century Danish king named Harald Gormsson. Gormsson united Scandinavia and converted the Danes to Christianity. His nickname was Bluetooth, a reference to a dead tooth that had turned blue. In the 1990s, Bluetooth became the name for the wireless area networking standard we use today.

In the sixth color, *Pink Goldfish* (co-authored with David Rendall) returned to the marketing roots of Purple. It examined differentiation and how to create competitive separation in business. Pink was inspired by David wearing head-to-toe pink both on and off stage.

The seventh color was Yellow. *Yellow Goldfish* (co-authored with Rosaria Cirillo Louwman) looked at how companies can do a little extra to contribute to the happiness of its customers, employees, and society. Yellow was inspired by the warmth of the sun and the yellow, smiling, happy face created by Harvey Ball in 1963 for a State Mutual Life Insurance advertisement.

The eighth color was Gray. *Gray Goldfish* (co-authored with Brian Doyle) examined how to navigate the gray areas of leading five different generations in the workforce: Matures, Boomers, Generation

X, Millennials, and Generation Z. It is no longer a "one-size-fits-all" leadership proposition.

The ninth color was literally a gem. The *Diamond Goldfish* (co-authored with Travis Carson and Tony Cooper) was about sales and client management. It explored how to excel under pressure and operate via the Diamond Rule in business. The use of Diamond was inspired by how the gem is created. To quote Henry Kissinger, "A diamond is a chunk of coal that did well under pressure."

The tenth color was Silver. There are three reasons for the second metal in the series. They are readability, conductivity, and polishability. The *Silver Goldfish* (co-authored with Alan Hoffler) is a guide for delivering memorable business presentations. It shares the 10 keys to being loud and clear when speaking.

That brings us to Red.

WHY RED?

Red is the color of blood. It's been historically associated with sacrifice and courage. In the US and Europe, red also represents passion, whereas in Asia, it symbolizes happiness and good fortune. Our inspiration for RED comes from Africa.

(RED) was created by Bono and Bobby Shriver. Launched at the World Economic Forum in 2006, its purpose was to engage the private sector and its marketing prowess in order to raise funds in the fight against AIDS in Africa. They outlined their idea for a unique union of brands and consumers on the back of a napkin. The plan had three goals:[13]

1. Provide consumers with a choice that made giving effortless

2. Generate profits and a sense of purpose for partner companies

---

13. http://www.wolffolins.com/work/37/red

3. Create a source of sustainable income for the Global Fund to fund the fight against AIDS.

(RED) was a continuation of work by U2's lead singer for Africa. In 2002, Bono co-founded DATA (Debt, AIDS, Trade, Africa), a platform to raise public awareness of the issues in its name and to influence government policy on Africa. In 2004, DATA helped to create ONE: The Campaign to Make Poverty History. ONE is dedicated to fighting extreme poverty and preventable disease. In early 2008, DATA and ONE combined operations under the ONE banner.

(RED) has a clear purpose seen in its manifesto:

> Every Generation is known for something.
>
> Let's be the one to deliver an **AIDS FREE GENERATION**.
>
> We all have tremendous power. What we choose to do or even buy, can affect someone's life on the other side of the world. When you BUY (RED), a (RED) partner will give up some of its profits to fight AIDS.
>
> It's as simple as that.
>
> BE (RED). Start the end of AIDS now.

Prior to the launch of (RED), businesses had contributed just $5 million to the Global Fund in four years. Since its inception, the private sector, through (RED), has contributed over $450 million. One hundred percent of the funds are invested in HIV/AIDS programs in Africa with a focus on countries with a high prevalence of mother-to-child transmission of HIV. (RED) supported grants have impacted more than 180 million lives.

The branding agency Wolff Olins created a unique brand architecture that united participating businesses by literally multiplying their logos to the power (RED). Global brands such as Apple, Nike, Dell, American Express, and The Gap became partners. The appeal of (RED) was clear: it allowed them to tap into a purpose beyond their own profit. Partner brands created special (RED) versions of products and a portion of the profits from the sales would contribute to the Global Fund to fight malaria, tuberculosis, and AIDS.

Here are some examples of (RED) initiative products:

- American Express Red card

- Gap's Product Red line of merchandise including T-shirts, jackets, scarves, gloves, jewelry, bags, and purses

- Apple Inc's special edition iPod Touch 5th generation and five other generations of iPod Nano and the iPod Shuffle as well as a (RED) $25 iTunes Gift Card

- Nike's special line of red shoelaces

- Hallmark's Product Red greeting cards

- In a partnership with Microsoft, Dell's XPS One, XPS M1530, and XPS M1530 computers with a PRODUCT (RED) version of Windows Vista Ultimate preinstalled

- Dell's PRODUCT (RED) printer

- Monster Cable's special edition of Beats by Dr. Dre

- Belvedere Vodka's special edition red-colored bottles

(RED) helped reinforce the simple idea that doing good is good business for both customers and employees. American Express saw an immediate lift in brand perception with younger customers, while GAP saw a major improvement in employee engagement, as well as the quality of incoming recruits. Their INSPI(RED) T-shirt became the biggest-seller in its history.

Starbucks was one of the very first (RED) partners. Here is how they describe the relationship:[14]

> We have deep relationships with many coffee grow-ing communities in Africa. Their health and prosper-ity are important to us, and we have an opportunity to help them thrive, and to use our size for good. One way we support our global communities is through our eight-year partnership with (RED) – thanks to you we've contributed more than $14 million and count-ing. All donations generated through (STARBUCKS) RED campaigns have gone to the Global Fund to help finance HIV/AIDS prevention, education, and treat-ment programs. The program is making a difference. There have been enormous gains in the fight against AIDS in the last decade, but also persistent challenges. We believe the elimination of mother to child trans-missions by 2020 and the end of AIDS as a public health threat by 2030 is possible, but only with con-tinued funding and focus. Without these efforts, the epidemic threatens to outpace the response and undo the progress that's been achieved.

The appeal of (RED) was clear. It connected organizations with a purpose beyond their own profit. Some partners went as far as manufacturing products or packaging in African countries, gener-ating jobs and opportunities for local people.[15]

14. https://www.starbucks.com/responsibility/community/starbucks-red

15. http://www.wolffolins.com/work/37/red

We are using the color red similarly. How are you going above and beyond the transaction to connect purpose to your promotional products?

Now, let's explore why a Goldfish.

CHAPTER 4

WHY A GOLDFISH?

"Big doors swing on little hinges"

- W. Clement Stone

The origin of the goldfish in *Red Goldfish* dates back to 2009 when the Purple Goldfish crowdsourcing project was started. It has become a signature part of this book series. A goldfish represents something small, but despite its size, something with the ability to make a big difference.

The inspiration for the goldfish came from Kimpton Hotels. Introduced at the Hotel Monaco in 2001, the boutique hotel chain began to offer travelers the ability to adopt a temporary travel companion for their stay. Perhaps you were traveling on business and getting a little lonely. Or maybe you were with family and missing your family pet. Kimpton to the rescue. They'll give you a goldfish for your stay. They call the program *Guppy Love*. The goldfish has become a signature element of the Kimpton experience and has gained national attention.

"The Guppy Love program is a fun extension of our pet-friendly nature as well as our emphasis on indulging the senses to heighten the travel experience," says Steve Pinetti, Senior Vice President of Sales & Marketing for Kimpton Hotels and Restaurants, of which Hotel Monaco is a premier collection. "Everything about Hotel Monaco appeals directly to the senses, and 'Guppy Love' offers one more unique way to relax, indulge and promote health of mind, body, and spirit in our home-away-from-home atmosphere."

Guppy Love inspired the start of the Purple Goldfish Project. Three years later in 2012, the book *Purple Goldfish* was published. The size of a goldfish was relevant to the series. The overarching concept is the idea that little things can make the biggest difference. The growth of a goldfish became a metaphor for business. The average common goldfish is between three to four inches in length (10 cm), yet the largest in the world is almost six times that size. Imagine walking down the street and bumping into someone 30 feet tall

(9 meters). How can there be such a disparity between a regular goldfish and their monster cousins? It turns out that the growth of the goldfish is determined by five distinct factors. Like goldfish, not all businesses will grow equally. The growth of a business is similar to that of a goldfish.

The growth of a goldfish and the growth of your organization is affected by the following five factors:

#1. Size of the Environment = The Market

GROWTH FACTOR: The size of the bowl or pond.

RULE OF THUMB: Direct correlation. The larger the bowl or pond, the larger the goldfish can grow. The smaller the market, the lesser the growth.

#2. Number of Goldfish = Competition

GROWTH FACTOR: The number of goldfish in the same bowl or pond.

RULE OF THUMB: Inverse correlation. The more goldfish, the less growth. The less competition, the more growth opportunity.

#3. The Quality of the Water = The Economy

GROWTH FACTOR: The clarity of the water and the level of nutrients in the water.

RULE OF THUMB: Direct correlation. The more nutrients and better clarity, the larger the growth. The less access to capital or reduced consumer confidence, the more difficult it is to grow.

Sidebar: Fact

A malnourished goldfish in a crowded, cloudy environment may only grow to two inches (five centimeters).

#4. Their first 120 days of life = Startup Phase or Product Launch

GROWTH FACTOR: The nourishment and treatment they receive as a baby goldfish.

RULE OF THUMB: Direct correlation. The lower the quality of the food, water, and treatment, the more the goldfish will be stunted for future growth. The stronger the leadership and capital as a start-up, the better the growth.

Fact - A baby goldfish is called a fry. They are tiny when they are born, literally a "small fry."

#5. Genetic Makeup = Differentiation

GROWTH FACTOR: The genetic makeup of the goldfish.

RULE OF THUMB: Direct correlation. The poorer the genes or the less differentiated, the less the goldfish can grow. The more differentiated the product or service from the competition, the better the chance for growth.

Fact - The current *Guinness Book of World Records* holder for the largest goldfish is from the Netherlands at a lengthy 19 inches (50 centimeters). To put that in perspective, that's the size of the average domestic cat.

Which of the five factors can you control?

Let's assume you have an existing product or service and have been in business for more than four months. Do you have any control over the market, your competition, or the economy? NO, NO, and NO. The only thing you have control over is your business's genetic makeup or how you differentiate your product or service.

It is our belief that purpose is becoming the ultimate differentiator. How are you becoming for-purpose in your business? In goldfish terms, how are you standing out in a sea of sameness?

CHAPTER 5

COMMITMENT, NOT A CAMPAIGN

"If you want to be successful, be willing to do things that other people won't do."

- Rory Vaden

Choosing purpose as a business practice is fraught with danger. For the latter part of the 2010s, social media became the land of "the Woke"—those willing to point out apparent hypocrisies, gender and racial biases, and other unacceptable behavior from the comfort of their smartphone. While statistical evidence supports the existence of an opportunity to connect with emerging buyer demographics using purpose as a strategy, there is considerable evidence to suggest that consumers are not only wary of insincere efforts, they've actually weaponized the court of public opinion to work against the perpetrator, often at the peril of sales results, dividend performance, and ultimately, the reputation of those brands seeking to connect using purpose.

The nature of trust has changed

Trust: Competence and ethics
Trust today is granted on two distinct attributes: competence (delivering on promises) and ethical behavior (doing the right thing and working to improve society). Currently, no one institution is considered both competent and ethical.

(no institution seen as both competent and ethical, competence score, net ethical score)

Trust moves local
Trust has moved from a top-down vertical model, dependent on traditional leaders, to to a horizontal one, in which people rely more on friends, family, and "a person like me."

Top-down trust
People trust or distrust in response to the decisions and messages of authority figures

The dynamic shifts in trust
How the vectors of trust have changed over two decades

Horizontal trust
People trust or distrust based on their interaction with a peer, or "a person like me"

Local trust
People trust or distrust based on their interaction with others who are personally close to them in their community, workplace, or family

Source: Richard Edelman, *Edelman Trust Barometer*

As referenced in the above graphic, courtesy of Richard Edelman, author of the *Edelman Trust Barometer*, you can see consumer behavior and trust has shifted away from a top-down approach, where people were seen to trust or distrust directly as the result of belief (or the absence of belief) in authority figures and toward a more local version of trust, where people choose to trust or distrust based on input from friends, family, and others who "look like me."

Also of note are the foundational elements that comprise trust: competence (delivering on promises) and ethical behavior (doing the right thing and working to improve society). As these elements of trust emerge, it's increasingly important for businesses to be able to communicate how they are walking their talk.

That being said, if you're still up for the challenge, there are ways to navigate these perilous, trust-barren seas.

The size of your organization will often dictate how best to begin the process of aligning on purpose. Working in tandem with employees creates the best opportunity for long term success, but examining opportunities for alignment in the boardroom among the executive/ownership/leadership team often serves as a substitute. While it's still better to have a plan with many stakeholders participating, it's more important to begin than it is not to begin out of fear of a lackluster start, so if your efforts need to begin with the executive team only, in most instances that's better than not starting at all.

We'll examine prescriptive ways to execute on getting started later in the book. The most important consideration in this exercise is authenticity. You can't manufacture your desire to get behind something as a means to fool people into giving you their money. You have to have a sincere desire to build (or in most instances, remodel) your business to be a clearer reflection of what and who the people behind your business are all about.

Once you've hammered out how you intend to start, it's vital that you make these efforts part of your business planning process. Devoting time and attention to the development, implementation, and measurement of your progress should be a part of your strategic planning efforts. By committing your efforts to the written parts of your business, you'll remain attuned to the day-to-day activities necessary to demonstrate your newly crafted purpose-driven status. With repetition comes improvement and consistent repetition requires commitment, a commitment that often will fade with time when not made a foundational aspect of the business plan.

Standing out in a sea of sameness requires focused attention on creating and fostering a differentiation strategy. By developing the purpose behind your business and committing to the activities that come along with doing so, you're building a well-positioned differentiation strategy, a strategy that has consistently and repeatedly been shown to out-perform the marketplace. It's not simple to execute, and many businesses have made unsuccessful attempts to align on purpose, but those that are successful, report results that would make any entrepreneur gleeful. The nature of the work changes when viewed through a purpose-driven lens, but the business outcomes have a tendency to be memorable when driven from a place of purpose.

Competitive differentiation was already a difficult proposition in the pre-COVID-19 economy, but a record-setting run of prosperity covered up a number of glaringly obvious problems that have been laid bare with an economy returned to the starting gate:

1. Many business owners started their business in the time since the 2008 Great Recession. They haven't experienced this type of economic downturn and have no experience in handling the realities of a constrained marketplace.

2. A booming economy created jobs for almost everyone. When there's sufficient work to keep EVERYONE busy, the need to stand out from your competitors is mitigated.

3. Generational differences between late-career Baby Boomers and ambitious Millennials was already creating tension in the workplace, tension that has now morphed and grown with added layers of socioeconomic and racial tensions facing the American public. (Stan Phelps and Brian Doyle do

a masterful job covering this generational concern in *Gray Goldfish*.)

As we move to the post-pandemic portion of our economic rebirth, it will be of specific interest to watch how the predictions made in the Richard Edelman graphic presented at the beginning of the chapter happen in each of our communities. It's interesting to witness the localization of spending that can be seen in a robust open-air farmers market thriving in the face of the pandemic as shoppers seek more COVID-19 friendly environments to buy food coupled with a renewed interest in knowing where the products being bought were grown. Nothing like the farmer herself selling her produce to be sure of its origin.

Will emerging forces—like businesses aligning on purpose in the aftermath of all that's occurred since January 1, 2020—be able to reverse the clear and obvious signs of peril that accompany a lack of competitive differentiation? We can be sure of more scarce resources for a prolonged period of time, likely dating well into 2021, and we are waiting for a credible vaccine to be developed. Will businesses aligned on purpose be able to reap a fast-start competitive advantage as the new economy presents itself?

There are a lot of unanswered questions at this point, but one thing is clear; there will be heightened expectations for brands and organizations. Businesses able to meet those expectations, or better yet, exceed them, not only will cement their brand in consumer hearts and pocketbooks, they will champion a cause to all who will listen.

In the pages to come, we spotlight the ways purpose-driven businesses in the Promotional Marketing industry are doing their work, the ways those businesses are positively impacting the community, the environment, and humanity, and we investigate the many forms purpose takes when buyers of promotional marketing items activate good deeds with their purchases.

SECTION II:

THE ARCHETYPES
(THE WHAT)

CHAPTER 6

GIVE BACK

"If you want to succeed at the concept of a give-first economy you have to give without any expectation of something in return. The irony is, when you authentically and sincerely give, you have a tendency to get more back in return."

— Kirby Hasseman

We started the *Red Goldfish Project* in 2015. Since its origination, we've collected information on over 500 organizations for *Red Goldfish, Red Goldfish Nonprofit Edition,* and *Red Goldfish Promo Edition,* specifically looking for ways that brands bring purpose to life. Our research database includes over 700 articles and nearly 3,000 videos. [See the original collection of videos searchable by brand, archetype, and chapter at http://602communications.com/RedGoldfish]

In reviewing all of the companies, we began to see patterns. We saw that brands would typically fall into one of eight archetypes.

Here are the original eight purpose archetypes we discovered:

1. **The Protector** - Those who protect what is important.

   Example: Patagonia. Their purpose is to help reimagine a sustainable world for those who come after us.

2. **The Liberator** - Those who reinvent a broken system.

   Example: Harley Davidson. Their purpose is to fulfill dreams of personal freedom through the experience of motorcycling.

3. **The Designer** - Those who empower through the creation of revolutionary products.

   Example: Apple. Their purpose is to make tools for the mind that advance humankind.

4. **The Guide** - Those who help facilitate individual progress.

   Example: Google. Their purpose is to organize the world's information and make it universally accessible.

5. **The Advocate** - Those who advocate for a tribe.

   Example: Panera. Their purpose is to help people live consciously and eat deliciously.

6. The Challenger - Those who inspire people toward trans-formative action.

Example: Nike. Their purpose is to inspire every athlete . . . and if you have a body, you are an athlete.

7. The Commander - Those who command individuals to join a movement.

Example: Whole Foods. Their purpose is to set the standards of excellence for food retailers.

8. The Master - Those on a mission to change lives and improve the world.

Example: Warby Parker. Their purpose is to offer designer eyewear at a revolutionary price while leading the way for socially conscious businesses.

For *Red Goldfish Promo Edition,* we dissected over 250 case studies. We determined that there are five categories where promotional products can leverage purpose to increase engagement and impact. We'll share examples of each over the next five Chapters. Here are the five types:

1. Give Back

2. Diversity & Inclusion

3. Environmental

4. Experience

5. Transparency & Trust

Let's go . . .

GIVE BACK

"From what we get, we can make a living;
what we give, however, makes a life."

— Arthur Ashe

The prevalence of Buy One, Give One programs and other initiatives where for-profit businesses make a financial contribution in the form of a percent of revenue sold or as a dollar-for-dollar matching partner for employee contributions to a cause has exploded in occurrence and popularity in the last decade. The financial benefit of cause marketing has grown and is estimated to be upwards of $2.2 billion. It's not difficult to find an example in grocery store or retail aisles these days, and celebrities like U2's Bono have lent their influence with great success to initiatives like The (RED) Campaign, bringing attention to and awareness for additional resources to be dedicated to eliminating global health risks in underserved areas.

As is the case with most B2C behavior, businesses find themselves organizing around causes and communicating their commitment in equal parts to establish for their employees a sense of what the company they work for cares about and is willing to support as well as establish an emotional connection with those buying the products they sell. By aligning behind a cause or some other aspirational objective, these organizations are reading the tea leaves of the sentiment behind the buying practices of the customers they most covet and arranging their organizational objectives to better reflect these changes in consumer sentiment, fueled largely by emerging generations of buyers led by Generation Z (Gen Z) and late-stage Millennials.

Gen Z has proven to be tremendously tuned in to the concept of businesses aligned on purpose. Statistics report 93 percent of Gen Z say that a company's impact on society affects their decision to work there, and 30 percent of Gen Z would take a 10 to 20 percent pay cut to work for a company with a mission they deeply care about. Further, 69 percent of this group are more likely to buy from a company that contributes to social causes, while 33 percent have stopped buying from a company that contributes to a cause with which they disagree. The statistics in these categories repeatedly suggest Gen Z to be the MOST aligned on purpose and MOST interested in aligning using purpose as the filter of choice. These consumers don't want to merely buy from a company, they want to become PART of the brand.

Companies choosing to align on purpose are betting that the emotional connection prospective consumers feel for a cause will be strong enough to compel purchasers to make theirs the brand of choice in their category. By tapping into an already strong emotional connection, brands attempt to piggyback on that consumer sentiment by virtue of emotional association. Studies suggest a strong correlation between consumer willingness to change brands and the presence of a tie to causes those consumers care about.

Virtually no business operates in a marketplace absent competition, and there can only be one low-cost provider in each market. The remainder must choose another key value for purchasers, resulting in an often crowded, noisy, difficult marketplace with countless choices for prospective buyers and little in the way of apparent differentiation of choice.

Branded Merchandise businesses—Suppliers, Distributors, and Service Providers—have also recognized this possibility in our marketplace. While we will examine a number of available purpose-driven categories in the pages to come, we have found charity and donation vehicles the enthusiastically and overwhelmingly selected choice for communicating what businesses choose to stand up for.

Because ours is a physical medium representing product categories identical to what's available in the retail marketplace, many of the factories manufacturing products for the branded merchandise industry manufacture those same products for retail.

As those factories witnessed growth in retail demand for products they manufacture once a give-back component was added, it was only natural they would share that intelligence with their branded merchandise product buyers. A massive demand for the Yeti product line fueled a noteworthy spike in corporate buyer requests to co-brand their company logo with well-known retail brands. This presented a unique opportunity for the branded merchandise marketplace to adopt similar giving strategies for products bound for corporate buyers.

And boy did they. We gathered countless case studies in preparation for writing this book. The quantity of examples in this category far outweighed any other category. We've found broad sub-type categories within this giving strategy where donation and charity-based efforts were focused:

1. Buy One, Give Some programs

2. Percent of company sales programs

3. Direct product donation programs

4. Product-based fundraising programs

Here are some of the best and most interesting examples we found:

PEERLESS UMBRELLA

Buy One, Give Some

Founded in 1927, originally as a parachute company, the third-generation family-owned Peerless Umbrella designs and manufactures its lifetime-guaranteed umbrellas in its New Jersey facility. The family feel of the organization is best exemplified by the 40-year average employee tenure. Once people join the Peerless team, they rarely leave. It's a paragon of a thriving culture with happy employees. Dan Edge, current Peerless President, leads with his heart, and internal and external clues are easily found.

Internal

- On a chosen Friday each October, for each pink-clad employee Dan donates $20 to a local breast cancer foundation in honor of his mother.

- Toy and coat drives are annual events in their facility, along with food drives for the area community.

External

- Threads of Hope: Clearance products are earmarked with a $1 donation for St. Jude's Children's Research Hospital. Peerless made donations of $2,500 in 2018 and close to $5,000 in 2019. As the program's popularity has grown, Peerless has expanded the non-profit partner options to allow purchasers of the branded product to direct the donation to a non-profit of their choice. By allowing the buyer to direct the donation, Peerless imbues the purchase with greater emotion.

- Rainy Day Heroes: A chance Austin, Texas, encounter with a member of the local homeless community inspired National Account Manager Charity Gibson to lobby the company to begin a dedicated program of umbrella donation as a part of their everyday business activities.

  Charity said, "While the plight of the homeless is heart-breaking, it's hope-giving to know that people can absolutely cherish something as simple as a $4 [or] $5 umbrella."

  In this program, promotional marketing consultants apply for boxes of free Peerless umbrellas, with the promise that the free umbrellas make their way into the community as a donation to those in need of the protection and comfort an umbrella provides.

  What started from this chance encounter has become a social media sensation. Many feeds are populated with heartwarming scenes of giving as those free umbrellas make their way into the hands of those for which the program was intended. Peerless has garnered media attention as a result of these efforts, and they've won more than their fair share of new clients as a result of the increased visibility and the emotional reactions from those successfully executing on the program.

Charity said, "The most rewarding part is when the promotional consultants send us back pictures and videos of them handing out umbrellas, especially the one woman who videoed her 3-year-old daughter handing out umbrellas, screaming "Can HE have one, Mommy?"

MPOWERED

Buy Some, Give One Program

MPOWERD is a unique acronym:

Micro: Create simple, portable, and personal products

POWER: Provide clean technology to expand opportunities

Design: Combine form and function in all products

In 2012, MPOWERED created Luci, the first inflatable solar light with the goal of making an affordable clean energy product that people could use in any situation. This Certified B Corporation was founded in the heart of New York City. While their product is lights, their mission is to empower the lives of 1.5 billion people living without electricity in low-income countries.

MPOWERED uses the power of business to build a more inclusive and sustainable economy. Their Give Luci Program donates lights to their partners—a sustainable business model that means the more product sold domestically, the more affordable they can sell to emerging markets and emergency response situations.

Chief Business Development Officer and Founder John Salzinger, a native New Yorker and born entrepreneur, launched MPOWERD with the idea that innovative companies have a responsibility to lead, not only in the marketplace but as a real force for good.

Salzinger had this to say about the role his business intends to play in the economy, "I'm pleased that the private sector is taking the opportunity to care about people and the planet. It's not being done by the people who were tasked to do so, so it's up to us to do the job."

MPOWERD CEO Seungah Jeong brings a unique background and perspective to the mission. As a child, Seungah lived in a South Korean home with no electricity or running water. They used kerosene lanterns as their only available light source, a dangerously volatile, noxious, and highly flammable means to provide light. Her childhood experience served as motivation for her career in environmental development and sustainability.

MPOWERD works with over 700 NGOs and nonprofits, providing clean energy to those who need it most. They distribute clean energy options that provide a more economical and environmentally friendly approach to everyday tasks. They sent more than 100,000 lights to Puerto Rico following the two recent natural disasters that struck the island. The company has touched more than 4,000,000 lives and averted more than 2 million tons of CO2.

The organization has a loyal and devoted user following. The lifestyle photography seen splashed across their brand is user-generated content. By creating opportunities for their product to do its intended job as donations to emerging economies, ambassadors supply the company with a seemingly endless stream of photographic proof of how its products are actually used in real life, both in emerging economies and the developed world.

It's clear that MPOWERD has created a brand that awakens a sense of participation in something greater than ourselves, a key trigger in successful marketing. By tying emotion to their cause, MPOWERD has developed a more intimate relationship with their followers, as evidenced by the user community's willingness to help market the brand independent of John or Seungah.

Activities in this category continued into the Shelter in Place period of the global pandemic. Many factories in the Promotional Marketing industry began PPE production to meet the exploding demand for products by frontline workers and healthcare professionals. Let's look at some examples:

REDWOOD CLASSICS

Buy One, Give One

This Ontario-based apparel supplier donated thousands of masks to hospitals and charities. Redwood pivoted their manufacturing early in the COVID-19 crisis to mask production, selling ready-made and DIY mask kits to the public. With each mask purchased, Redwood committed to donating a mask to those working on the frontlines—in the health-care community, caretakers, grocery store employees, restaurant workers, truck drivers, delivery people, and essential service providers.

"It's a privilege to give back to the city and country that has given our family business so much," says Kathy Cheng, president and founder of Redwood Classics. "In a world where we celebrate technology, and how quickly that technology can be adapted, our silver lining is the ability to transform our factory into a mask-production house until regular factory activities can resume."

The Company and its volunteer skeleton crew of craftspeople and support staff produced and donated thousands of masks to local health-care facilities and organizations, including Michael Garron Hospital, Mount Sinai Hospital, Chai Lifeline Canada, and Moose Cree First Nation. The response was so enormous that the Redwood Classics team had to add a donation request portal to its website.

STORM CREEK

Buy One, Give One

Buy One, Give One

1. Order a pullover for yourself, checkout and pay online.
2. Watch for your order confirmation email – there will be a link to an order form for your HERO's free pullover.
3. Fill out that form, select the gender, size and color of pullover for your HERO. We ship your gift and note to them for FREE!

Storm Creek, another industry apparel supplier, also launched a Buy One Give One campaign for consumers to support essential heroes working on the front lines of COVID-19. The Wear for Better Collection consisted of jersey quarter-zip pullovers for men and for women, featuring a logo that recognizes a variety of essential worker occupations from medical staff to grocers, restaurant workers, farmers, bankers, teachers, childcare providers, and more, along with the words "Together We Fight."

For every pullover purchased, customers could choose an essential worker in their life to receive the same item free of charge along with a personalized note. There are multiple versions of the logo available in addition to the NYC-themed log in the picture—one with the logo of the state of Minnesota and another with an American flag.

"The overall theme of the campaign is 'wear with hope, wear with courage, wear with love, wear with all,'" said Storm Creek co-owner Theresa Fudenberg. *"The collection serves as a unique and personal way for everyone to wear their support, literally, for the heroes who are working to keep us all safe. We look forward to thanking and outfitting many essential heroes in our community and beyond."*

It's no surprise promotional marketing companies offered their products to the benefit of society during this time of crisis. The marketplace has long rallied to the aid of those in need—the global pandemic provided us the perfect opportunity to demonstrate that willingness once again, and we rose to the occasion. Many who call this industry home have much to be proud of, and while we consider how the financial landscape has been altered, it was clear in the interim that we were not only willing to help but to link arms and work together to bring resources to our communities.

While in-kind product is a popular way of demonstrating willingness to give, percent of sales options are also an equally prevalent and accepted way of showing your giving heart. Here are some examples of how it works:

HIRSCH GIFT PATRIOT

Percent of Sales

Based in Houston, Texas, Hirsch Gift has a long history of helping others. Founder Peter Hirsch was awarded the Bess Cohn Humanitarian of the Year award for 2018 as recognized by the Advertising Specialty Institute for his and his company's efforts to assist in the aftermath of both Hurricane Katrina in New Orleans in 2005 and then Harvey in his hometown in 2017. Following Hurricane Harvey, his company staff organized and transported over 200 pallets of necessities contributed by members of the Promotional Marketing industry to community distribution points like schools and churches.

Peter said, "When it comes to something like a disaster, you have to draw on friendships and relationships. There's a deep level of trust because when somebody sends you a 40-foot container of towels from across the country, they want to make sure it goes to a worthy cause."

The Company's willingness to contribute extends to the products they sell. Products in the company's Patriot line feature 20 percent of net proceeds donated to Homes for Our Troops (HFOT). The organization's tagline, "Building Homes, Rebuilding Lives," is personified by the services offered—specially adapted custom homes nationwide for severely injured post-9/11 veterans. HFOT builds these homes where the veteran chooses to live and continues its relationship with the veterans after home delivery to assist them with rebuilding their lives. To date, the non-profit has built over 270 homes. In a little more than 18 months, sales of Patriot products have resulted in the donation of more than $60,000 by Hirsch Gift to Homes for Our Troops.

Referring to a card he had received from a Homes for Our Troops beneficiary, Peter said, "It's things like this that make what we do so important. The more Patriot product we collectively sell, the more we're able to help people like the young man that sent us this note. I've never [before] seen the sense of cooperation inherent in the Promotional Marketing industry, it's fantastic and it needs to be fostered."

During COVID-19, Hirsch Gift has added a mask to its line of products in support of their 20 percent of net proceeds commitment for all Patriot products.

RECTOR COMMUNICATIONS

Product-Based Fund Raising Program

Founded in 2008, Screenbroidery was named *Counselor Magazine's* 2012 Fastest Growing Company by the Advertising Specialty Institute and recognized in 2018's Best Places to Work List. When the national economy was idled as a result of shutdown orders mandated due to the COVID-19 outbreak, Screenbroidery sales increased by 200 percent.

Tom Rector, Screenbroidery founder, self-identifies as a hustler and that hustler mentality is pervasive within Screenbroidery culture. With the economy largely shuttered, Tom and his staff felt the urge to do something to be supportive of the businesses in their Indianapolis economy. The resulting #DoYourPart program served as a fundraising vehicle for the less fortunate when 100 percent of the profits from the sale of T-shirts emblazoned with COVID-19 themed sayings like "United by Isolation" and "Quarantine & Chill" were transformed into gifts cards from local small businesses and then donated to the United Way of Central Indiana and the COVID-19 Community Economic Relief Fund. The gift cards were distributed through local community centers directly to those individuals and families in need. Local and national news media took interest in the program.

Said Tom, "Everyone wants to be part of the solution. Unless you're a front-line worker, there wasn't a lot many of us could do. People were looking for a sense of hope and the ability to be able to connect and provide some part of a solution. This was an easy way monetarily where folks could participate."

THE DUNSTON GROUP

Product-Based Fundraising

Based in Charlotte, North Carolina, The Dunstan Group has been a bedrock of the local community since the company's inception in 2008. The Dunstan Group's approach to community is right on their website:

> "Here at The Dunstan Group, we've seen how one person can make a big difference in the community. Start adding more people, families, and businesses to that equation, and the difference made is even bigger. That's the simple math behind why we feel working with not-for-profit and community-based organizations is more than just good business, it's great for our hometown, too."

Examples of their community-minded approach color much of their work, as many non-profit organizations promote The Dunstan Group and their work in appreciation for the numerous ways the company aids nonprofits in increasing their reach. Here's a case study of one such instance.

> 24 Foundation is a non-profit organization close to The Dunston Group founder Scott Dunstan's heart. Since 2002, the Charlotte-based charity has raised more than $21 million to support cancer navigation and improve quality of life and survivorship for cancer patients. Its signature events bring cyclists, walkers, survivors, families, and friends together for 24-hour tests of endurance, remembrance, community, and celebration.

The Challenge:

In honor of his mother's memory, Scott started riding in 24 Hours of Booty, the Foundation's signature cycling and fundraising event. As the years progressed, many more people dear to him were affected by cancer, including two close friends who lost children to pediatric cancer. In 2009, The Dunstan Group became the supplier of the 24 Foundation's branded merchandise.

As the event grew and branched out to other cities, the message of fundraising for the important work of cancer navigation had to be consistent on all platforms across the country with cool fundraising incentives, comfortable riding gear, staff shirts, volunteer shirts, fundraising awards, and branded merchandise for the 24 Foundation support store.

The Big Idea:

Each fall The Dunstan Group works with the marketing and branding teams at the 24 Foundation to identify unique product, apparel, and designs that can help them excite participants, reach their fundraising and awareness goals, and provide long-lasting branding appeal. From a fundraising perspective, a high-quality incentive item may provide a tipping point for participants to make one more ask, send one more email, and reach that "next level." The 24 Foundation's two annual events are also supported by on-brand apparel, gear, and other goods that are available through the program's online store.

The merchandise provided for the 2019 24 Hours of Booty included 20 unique branded items from pens and bracelets to bamboo sunglasses, hair ties, and even cowbells!

The Reaction:

"The 24 Foundation developed into the hugely impactful non-profit it is today because of partnerships with like-minded individuals like Scott Dunstan and The Dunstan Group," says Katy Ryan, Executive Director of the 24 Foundation. "Scott and his team are true partners. Each year, Scott participates in the event, raises funds on behalf of the organization, and helps us create a successful road map for recruitment and retention through our apparel, incentives, and promo items."

"The personalized attention is what keeps drawing 24 Foundation back to The Dunstan group year after year," says Ryan.

"The Dunstan Group always delivers more than expected each year, helping propel us forward as we seek to expand and improve upon our mission to provide cancer navigation and survivorship for all. This is why we always choose the Dunstan team. They care not just about what we do, but why we do it."

By adopting a kindness-centered philosophy, businesses like those featured in this section continue to report performance that outpaces the success of other organizations in their categories. They report better employee retention rates, and these motivated employees drive the dynamic increases in sales witnessed by these businesses.

During the Shelter and Place period of 2020, most consumers found themselves with an embarrassment of riches from a free-time perspective, and the result was predictable—everyone went straight to the internet where nearly every form of entertainment available is shifting to a digital delivery method. Netflix alone reported the addition of nearly 16 million new accounts in Q1 2020.

The Shelter in Place period gave brands a unique opportunity to connect with consumers on a personal level with some brands going to great lengths to deliver their message in a meaningful way. *Ad Age* even went so far as to create a website dedicated solely to chronicling the ways brands reacted to the situation. Here is a cross-section of companies displaying their giving hearts during the pandemic.

COTTONELLE

Given the rate at which stores were selling out of product, one of the world's largest toilet paper producers, Cottonelle, delivered a direct message to ease consumers' concerns and discourage panic buying. Instead, the brand urged people to "stock up on generosity" and simultaneously launched a campaign called #ShareASquare in partnership with the US-based charity United Way.

The brand pledged $1 million and one million rolls of toilet paper to United Way Worldwide's COVID-19 Community Response and Recovery Fund. And for everyone who used the hashtag #ShareASquare, the brand donated an additional $1 up to $100K.

"We believe our consumers have no shortage of kindness," said Arist Mastorides, family care president at Cottonelle's parent company, Kimberly Clark North America. "So we trust that they will #ShareASquare to help us on this mission."

GUINNESS

While St. Patrick's Day is normally a tentpole moment for Guinness, the brand recognized the day would need to be different this year in support of bar closures and restrictions on social gatherings in Ireland and worldwide. Still, Guinness knew adults around the world needed a lift, so they responded with a message of resilience and assurance. By piecing together existing footage in a matter of days, Guinness shared that their own brand had endured the test of time by "sticking together."

With that in mind, they encouraged people to celebrate the spirit of the holiday by lifting one another just as they would lift a glass. "As a 260-year-old brand that has survived two World Wars, the Great Famine, and so much more, we felt compelled to share a message of resilience to reassure consumers that we will all march again if we stand together," explained Joey Converse, a senior brand manager at Guinness. To show their solidarity, the company committed $1 million to the Guinness Gives Back Fund, supporting their extended community and hospitality workers.

DOVE

Dove ran a touching video campaign titled Courage Is Beautiful featuring the exhausted faces of healthcare workers fresh from hours behind masks and other PPE that are clearly not only uncomfortable but, in some instances, capable of leaving lasting marks. The campaign was clearly well done and an emotional powerhouse. It resulted in contributions exceeding $5 million dollars around the globe. Dove earmarked $2 million for non-profit Direct Relief to provide PPE, ventilators, and medicine for healthcare workers on the frontlines of the fight against the virus.

Dove's parent company, Unilever, points to its "sustainable living plan," which the company says is being applied to many of its 400 brands. The purpose behind this plan is limiting environmental damage and helping people improve their health and wellbeing. Another purpose-oriented initiative was a threat to withdraw its advertising from platforms such as Facebook and Google in 2018 if those companies failed to eradicate extremist content that "create[d] division in society and promote[d] anger and hate."

While those examples were happening in the direct to consumer marketplace, the Promotional Marketing industry pitched in with countless businesses getting involved. Below are a few of the note-worthy examples of Suppliers and Distributors making contributions to the health and safety of their communities during the pandemic.

SHOWDOWN DISPLAYS

Supplier Showdown Displays, in Brooklyn Center, Minnesota, was named an essential business and in the process went to great lengths to re-engineer their production lines to make PPE products. The company produced medical gowns, protective screens, and masks, all of which were donated to local medical facilities to assist in their preparedness.

EAGLE PROMOTIONS

Distributor Eagle Promotions in Las Vegas, Nevada, donated 20,000 disposable masks and 1,500 KN95 FDA-approved masks. "Our team at Eagle Promotions is pleased to assist with the need and provide protective masks for our health-care workers, first-responders and nonprofit organizations," announced Eagle Promotions CEO Sean Ono and President Mario Stadtlander. "We are proud to collabo-rate with the Mask Task Force, powered by the Las Vegas Fashion Council, to help our community fight against the pandemic."

The Las Vegas Fashion Council's Mask Task Force was assembled to address the dire news of a mask shortage in the COVID-19 crisis and to support front-line medical and health workers, senior cen-ters, food banks, CCSD food distribution volunteers, and others. It has donated more than 5,000 masks to the Las Vegas community because of generous support of volunteers and sponsors like Eagle Promotions.

DISCOUNT MUGS

Discount Mugs, based in Medley, Florida, has partnered with IMC Health Medical Centers to donate 11,000 face masks to low-income seniors in Miami-Dade and Broward counties. The average age of recipients is 74 and most didn't have the means to buy the masks themselves.

The masks were be delivered to patients' homes along with instructions on how to safely use the mask and a contact number for any questions.

Next up are the powerful and dynamic ways businesses are connecting with their employees, the ways those employees help drive business success, and the ways those employers and employees together are making the world a better place.

CHAPTER 8

DIVERSITY / INCLUSION

"Diversity is being invited to the party; inclusion is being asked to dance."

– Verna Myers

D iversity incorporates all of the elements that make each individual unique. While there are infinite differences in humans, most of us subconsciously define diversity by a few social categories—gender, race, age, and so forth. SHRM defines inclusion separately from diversity as "the achievement of a work environment in which all individuals are treated fairly and respectfully, have equal access to opportunities and resources, and can contribute fully to the organization's success."

The branded merchandise supply chain is global. To compete for the marketing dollars spent on physical advertising items, sellers must price those products to approximate the cost a consumer would be charged to purchase the same item without a logo at retail. To satisfy that minimum requirement, branded merchandise factories and salespeople rely heavily on imported product to remain price-competitive, as we're able to leverage excess capacity in those factories making retail products to do the same for us at a fraction of the cost that would be required with a stand-alone supply chain of our own.

Because of the global nature of the supply chain for promotional products, it's historically been difficult for suppliers to properly vet their partners in factories often found more than halfway around the globe to audit and verify hiring practices as being respectful of the needs of all protected classes. Surges in demand for transparency and requests for certification of a safe, compliant, and inclusive supply chain have largely been driven by greater levels of scrutiny and attention from large corporate clients faced with their own supply chain certification needs combined with a growing consumer sentiment for ethically produced products from similarly ethical companies.

As is always the case in commerce, the marketplace has responded to these buyer demands. What's unusual in this instance, however, is the size distribution of businesses responding to the demand.

While large organizations like Sanmar, Hanes, and others have dedicated significant resources to the development and implementation of a more diverse and inclusive workforce, we've seen an increase in small, community-focused and outcome-based organizations entering the marketplace, boasting an array of impressive and unique employment constructs that find people of remarkable and unusual backgrounds working in interesting and unique businesses supporting the industry.

Here are a few examples of promotional marketing companies taking extraordinary approaches to their relationships with those that make the things these businesses sell.

HHPLIFT

Founded in 2007, Chicago-based HHPLIFT creates business through a combination of products sourced from other social enterprises and a workforce development program that supports and expands job opportunities for people with significant barriers to fair wage employment. They provide jobs themselves to Chicagoans from underserved communities by way of their attached nonprofit, the 1eleven Program.

As a self-proclaimed social enterprise, the 1eleven leadership and career development program is dedicated to breaking the cycle of poverty. In partnership with CARA, a premier Chicago-area workforce development organization, employees enjoy a sustainable wage, benefits, support services, and mentorship along with opportunities for educational and professional development. The intent is to provide support for the full human as opposed to what many would consider a more traditional employer/employee relationship.

As makers of handmade, high-quality bath and spa goods, HHPLIFT weaves a narrative around its employment practices that gives purchasers an added emotional jolt knowing their purchases not only will provide themselves a measure of self-care but at the same time will ensure the continued care of others making an attempt to break the cycle of poverty.

HHPLIFT's partners are supported with the financial contribution the organization makes in their products, but HHP vets their partners to ensure fair wages, safe working conditions, sustainability, and fair trade. Their partners span the globe with products manufactured in far-flung places like Cambodia, Guatemala, Sri Lanka, and Kenya.

Within the organization, 60 percent of participants have been promoted at least twice and the company has experienced a 225 percent increase in sales in a little over one year's time.

Inspired by a chance encounter with a bottle of Newman's Own salad dressing, HHPLIFT President Dena Hirshberg was awakened to the power of purpose in a for-profit business. When asked why she believed purpose as a business differentiator has grown in popularity in recent years, she commented:

> Increasingly over time, consumers are demanding that Companies they choose to buy from embrace Corporate Social Responsibility as a core value. More recently, as company employees are increasingly from Millennial and Gen Z demographics, these are the two-generational cohorts from whom Companies that embrace Corporate Social Responsibility and walk it like they talk it are going to recruit top talent, they're going to engage and motivate that top talent but most importantly, they're going to **retain** that top talent.

PACKED WITH PURPOSE (PwP)

A specialty gifting company with a social mission, Packed with Purpose curates personal gifts from social enterprises and purpose-driven companies, resulting in a more memorable gift that creates a positive community impact.

Founded in 2016, PwP creates custom gifts for businesses for a multitude of applications. The products that comprise these gift kits are sourced from an always evolving set of artisans affectionately known as *Purposeful Purveyors*. These Purposeful Purveyors represent a broad spectrum of community impact initiatives, providing job skills for young women, training for homeless youth, diverting waste from landfills, and offering new opportunities to the formerly incarcerated.

The company's commitment to its objective is pervasive. By organizing a list of partners around broad categories like the environment, workforce development, women's empowerment, youth development, and wellness, PwP creates opportunities for alignment between the message the gift giver wants to convey to recipients and those organizations from their partner list that best embody that message. In doing so, PwP delivers a powerful opportunity to create a positive emotional correlation in the mind of the gift recipient for its giver in a dizzying array of price points.

Aligning the recipient's gift and the causes they most care about through the choice of Purposeful Purveyors gains the opportunity to exponentially increase the value of the gift in the recipient's heart and mind and adds feelings of warmth for and alignment with the giver. With an impressive array of offerings available across the Purposeful Purveyor categories in the PwP program, gift-givers are opened to a never-before-seen array of ways to tell the story their gift is intended to convey.

While the story of each artisan in the PwP Purposeful Purveyors community is worthy of inclusion in this section, we've chosen five to highlight to serve as a cross-section of possibilities.

Detroit Food Academy

Detroit Food Academy works with local educators, chefs, and business owners to create food-related entrepreneurial experiences to inspire children and young adults. Whether it's cooking delicious, healthy meals for friends and family or developing artisanal food products, these experiences open doors, create connections, and spark confidence in Detroit's youth. As students transform their ideas into reality, they grow to become leaders who are connected, confident, and able to affect change.

Packed with Purpose offers Detroit Food Academy's Mitten Bites, all-natural, student-made snack bars packed with nutrition and flavor. These satisfying snacks come in six delicious flavors and contain no additives or preservatives. Sales of these delectable treats help create a stronger future for Detroit's youth.

Badala

Badala was started when founder Joelle McNamara, a restless and passionate high schooler, was struck with the realization that people were dying by the millions simply because they didn't have enough to eat. When she first traveled to Africa, she befriended women who were prostituting themselves just to feed their children. Instead of asking for handouts, everyone she met was looking for opportunities. Badala's line of housewares, jewelry, and accessories was born out of this request for employment.

Since launching in Kenya, the company has expanded their employment programs to women and artisans across East Africa and Central America and to domestic sex trafficking survivors. These houseware products provide employment and financial independence for women in poverty and survivors of trafficking. Products are also made with sustainably sourced wood from the region.

Kashwere

Kashwere's products support wellness efforts at both St. Jude's Children's Hospital and Colleen's Dream. Kashwere provides annual donations to fund St. Jude's work and also provides gifts for their annual Kid's Fashion Show. Through Colleen's Dream, velvety soft blankets are delivered monthly to women being treated for ovarian cancer, offering physical and emotional comfort during a stressful time.

Peaceful Fruits

Peaceful Fruits creates healthy snacks containing nothing but whole, organic fruit that is sustainably and ethically sourced. The company grew out of founder Evan Delahanty's work in the Amazon as a Peace Corps volunteer and now it works to sustain that rain forest by buying nearly all its fruit from the Amazon. This enables indigenous communities to harvest profitably, an essential element to saving the forests themselves.

At home, Peaceful Fruits helps people with developmental disabilities earn a fair wage by hiring them to fill nearly every position in the production of its snacks. To date, Peaceful Fruits has provided over 3,510 hours of full wage employment for people with disabilities and purchased 80,300 pounds of ethically sourced fruit, much of it helping to sustain the Amazon rainforest.

Resketch

Resketch journals are the most eco-friendly journal available. Resketch reduces waste by diverting interesting, usable paper away from landfills to create sketchbooks and notepads designed to foster creativity. They are made from a random assortment of high-quality, 100% reclaimed paper offering a different surface page after page. The paper is provided by companies ranging from award-winning architects to law offices.

The reclaimed paper doesn't go through a recycling process. Instead, it is used as it is found, always free of dirt and trimmed to journal size. Resketch believes that every sheet of paper has a story and wants to help inspire journalers to tell theirs.

Through partnerships with 108 Purposeful Purveyors, Packed with Purpose's 2019 results were impressive. They reported over 82,000 lives impacted across 23 states and 29 countries. Through the act of gifting, they helped provide over 13,000 hours of education, job training, and employment for youth and adults in underserved communities and supported farmers on over 250 acres of sustainably harvested farmland, the equivalent of 192 football fields.

SPECTRUM DESIGNS

Spectrum Designs, founded in 2011, is an operationally self-sustaining screenprint and embroidery facility in Pleasantville, New York. In conjunction with The Nicholas Center, it joins sister businesses, Spectrum Suds and Spectrum Bakes, in providing support for people with autism. Spectrum has grown at an explosive pace with sales increasing from $250,000 to more than $2,500,000. They count Special Olympics, Uber, and Google as customers.

By confronting head-on the reality that an estimated 70 to 90 percent of autistic adults are unemployed or underemployed, these businesses can also provide large companies with an avenue for corporate social outreach, mitigate the economic impacts on local communities for housing and caring for adults with autism, and provide hope for families that their children might have sustainable, relevant, and stimulating employment opportunities.

Spectrum COO Tim Howe said:

> The business model is successful for 2 main reasons:
>
> Compassion. People who wouldn't think twice about changing their screenprinter or embroiderer give us a shot based on compassion. If your life has been affected by Autism in any way, the notion of our business resonates with you.
>
> Guilt! It's not guilt from outside, it's guilt within the organization. By coming up with the model, we have positioned ourselves so that the quality of our work, the pricing, our ability to meet deadlines is not just a reflection of our business on its own, we're representing the abilities of everyone with a disability as a whole. It's a weighty expectation. We're out to prove that people with disabilities can do as good a job as people without disabilities, but in reality, you have to do a BETTER job so people will take notice. If you merely do as good a job as the alternative, if we fall into those traps, we'll lose the confidence of the customer. The weight and the guilt of a poor experience motivates us every day.

When asked to comment on the role giving back should make in decision-making for buyers choosing between options, Howe offered: "All things being equal, businesses are all adding value. If you're going to choose between two equal choices, I don't see a better thing to help you decide than what one company does philanthropically versus the other."

KNOTTY TIE

Founded in 2013 as a retail brand, Denver, Colorado's Knotty Tie shifted to promotional marketing in 2017. Resettled refugees comprise almost 50 percent of the employee roster. The company works each day to produce Knotty Tie's line of ties, scarves, pocket squares, and most recently, beautifully-crafted, fully-customizable masks.

Company founder Jeremy Priest had long been involved as a non-profit volunteer in the refugee community and identified an opportunity to create the supply chain that became the Knotty Tie product line. When the non-profit where he was a regular was not interested in the opportunity, Jeremy used $500 in available funds and a trip to Amazon.com for a sewing machine to implement his idea.

Today, Knotty Tie has 20+ employees doing jobs like graphic design, textile printing, laser cutting, cut & sew manufacturing, and fulfillment, all performed in a wide-open office environment. Their products are constructed of recycled materials, a nod to their desire to do what they do in a way that doesn't harm the planet.

In what is a recurring theme in this section of the book, we recognize a sincere effort among those companies in this category to reach for more than just the diversity and inclusion attributes that highlight their residence here. Their decision-making reflects a combination of purpose and commerce, of pulling together disparate pieces to make a seemingly brand-new collaboration among people from many walks of life, working together to create beautiful, well-constructed, and highly-technical products.

The characters behind the brands in this diversity and inclusion section of the book are all united by a passion for the causes and communities in which they've invested their resources. The results are noteworthy, and the stories are truly inspiring as these businesses often combine elements of many of the categories we're highlighting as foundational characteristics of purpose-driven businesses. The level of commitment demonstrated in these stories in many instances represents a personal emotional investment on the parts of the people featured. From Knotty Tie founder Jeremy Priest's recycled plastic garments made by refugees to Spectrum Designs teaching the world that the autistic can do meaningful work to Packed with Purpose founder Leatt Rothschild and HHP's president Dena Hirschberg creating ways to connect buyers with those most benefited by the dollars we spend, we witnessed an intense emotional connection to the outcomes these businesses champion.

This brings us to Ryan Moor, Ray DelMuro, and a group of passionate, caring members of our promotional marketing community doing amazing work in defense of the environment.

CHAPTER 9

ENVIRONMENTAL

"It is our collective and individual responsibility to preserve and tend to the world in which we all live."

– Dalai Lama

Promotional products are heavily reliant on the sale of items made from virgin plastic materials. Inexpensive to produce and relatively easy to transport from foreign ports, promotional products have long been seen as the "cheap marketing fix" for companies seeking a low-cost way to maintain visibility with consumers. Items made from plastic serve as the primary vehicle for purchasers to adorn with their logo to share with potential customers and clients.

Additionally, because of the ubiquitous nature of the ways these items can be purchased, promotional marketing items are frequently purchased without careful consideration of key success factors that would ensure the investment of logoed items did their intended job—provide brand recognition and create positive brand correlation for the recipient. It's in those instances where poorly chosen items have a tendency to end up in the waste stream. Visit any local convention center at the conclusion of a trade show or job fair and take a look at the garbage cans in and around the exits of the building for a stark example of the ways poorly chosen items don't execute on their intended result.

Dubbed "Brandfill," examples of poorly executed campaigns have led some to call for discontinuing the practice altogether, and while it's clear that changes in consumer sentiment with respect to honoring the environment and adopting less environmentally damaging business practices is driving marketplace reaction, how does a $25 billion dollar industry built largely on these potentially at-odds concepts create a way to be seen as something more than the historical and skin-crawling term of trinkets and trash?

Nothing like a global pandemic to change the narrative.

As the pandemic spread, the need for the items produced and sold by the Promotional Marketing industry made a hard turn in the direction of PPE manufacturing. As textiles are easily repurposed and many industry hard goods factories use the same equipment being used to manufacture other PPE items like face shields, many in our space retooled their manufacturing lines and worked day and night to make (and donate) hundreds of thousands of masks to frontline workers and healthcare heroes.

As our economy reopens, the knowledge and expertise gained by those factories in the manufacture of safe, compliant products worthy of the confidence of nervous consumers offers a potential avenue of escape for an otherwise hemorrhaging marketplace. The knowledge transfer from those manufacturers to their distributor representatives has been fueled by almost real-time communication among members of our industry, working in conjunction and collaboratively on social media platforms and in online discussions. There is a desire to have an impact on our community at a time of extreme need, exemplified by a long-held industry willingness to come together and solve problems for the benefit of the collective whole.

While much study will occur in the months and years following this global health threat, one of the clear realities of the Promotional Marketing industry in the years ahead is the need for alternative, reliable, and increasingly more local and sustainable choices. Consumers will want to know the faces they buy from and the reasons to support their choices. Increasingly this appears to be a vote for an organization's beliefs as much as its products. By focusing on creating a positive impact on the environment, businesses on both sides of the supply chain are banking on the scalability of that idea and the creation of business models that support practices that represent innovative reimagination of existing products, shift toward a closed-loop manufacturing system, attempt to diminish carbon footprints, and change packaging to create less waste and shipping costs.

In every instance, the businesses in this category approach their work with an acute sense of how best to make a positive impact on the environment, and in doing so, they offer the consumer an opportunity to support their efforts with the purchase of products and services they offer. There are a number of different ways business buyers can contribute toward environmental remediation. Programs supporting environmentally-focused non-profit organizations like 1% for the Planet and other causes we touched on in the Give Back section of the book represent more passive ways for buyers to support causes they believe in. In the upcoming pages we'll examine different approaches businesses have taken and their potential impact on the environment as a result.

In addition to companies repurposing product in creative ways, other companies within the promotional marketing marketplace have committed to reducing the size of their carbon footprint. Shipping products requires a fairly extensive amount of packaging, packaging that often is made from materials that are harmful to the environment. This preponderance of packaging creates additional weight in transit, further contributing to the negative environmental impact created when purchasing an order of branded merchandise, challenges being met head-on in thoughtful and creative ways by the companies found in this next section.

AAKRON LINE

Located in Buffalo, New York, and Chattanooga, Tennessee, family-owned Aakron Line has manufactured wood and plastic products like pencils and rulers since 1967. Employing more than 250 people, Aakron Line has supported NAEIR (The National Association for the Exchange of Industrial Resources) by way of a buy one, give one program from a cross-section of products from their catalog. Their support of the organization by way of this program spans over 20 years, making Aakron one of the longest supporters of a philanthropic program in our marketplace.

In 2020, second generation owners Devin Piscitelli and his sister Danielle doubled down on their commitment to make the world a better place with their attempts to minimize the company's carbon footprint. Devin said:

> We're very sensitive to the topic of our carbon footprint. On one hand, it's great, we're able to ensure that there are manufacturing jobs here in the U.S., which is something we're very proud of—one of the things we're most sensitive to is ensuring that all of our products are reusable in some way, not single use. We can sleep at night knowing that. One of the two ways we're limiting our carbon footprint as much as possible to start is with the polybags we use to package products. Anytime you buy a piece of drinkware or anything like that we use a polybag to protect the imprint from being scratched. As a result of this initiative, we are switching to biodegradable bags to do that job. We also use 100% post-consumer cardboard so together those efforts are our way of staying true to our stated desire to minimize our footprint.

It's noteworthy to recognize that many of the improvements being witnessed in carbon footprint reduction efforts are the result of an expanded set of options being offered by manufacturers of packaging products themselves. Historically, attempts to tackle packaging efforts were stymied more by the relative lack of availability of options and the associated costs of the few available options than a lack of desire on the part of the buyer of those packaging products. Only with increased demand has the marketplace flexed to accommodate those demands. After years of limited options, the scope of options from sustainable sources has started to grow.

VANTAGE APPAREL

In 1997, Ira Neaman started Vantage Apparel in Avenel, New Jersey. He has been a staunch advocate for the Promotional Marketing industry almost from day one, including his current role as 2020 Promotional Products Association International Chairman of the Board of Directors, the highest honor in industry volunteerism. He was the inaugural recipient of the PPAI Education Lifetime Achievement Award, and the Advertising Specialty Institute's *Counselor Magazine* named him their Person of the Year in 2003 and has included him in their ranking of the 50 most powerful industry members since 2008. Ira's influence within the industry has been vast, with multitudes of industry members benefitting from his knowledge and guidance.

As an apparel supplier, Vantage has long employed a strategy of interpreting retail fashion trends into their line to keep up with consumer demand and changing tastes. The result? Sales volume just north of $50 million annually places Vantage in the top 40 of suppliers in the Promotional Marketing industry.

Vantage's Earthwise line was released in 2020. This new line of men's and women's apparel items represented Vantage's first attempts to introduce garments manufactured from recycled products. While items in the line also see a contribution to water-based non-profit 1% for the Planet for each product sold, it's the use of a new fabric called Repreve that is the more noteworthy contribution to the environment. Repreve is a fabric woven from recycled plastic bottles into an extremely soft material that stands up to many trips to the washing machine and dryer, making the product incredibly valuable from a cost per use perspective. It could become the fabric for everyone's new favorite T-shirt.

In October 2019, 40 Vantage team members joined Clean Ocean Action for a beach clean-up day. They were among more than 40,000 people joining in an effort to remove hundreds of thousands of pounds of debris from New Jersey beaches

Clean Ocean Action consulted with Vantage at their New Jersey facility on ways for the day-to-day operations of the company to become more sustainable using the expansive Clean Ocean Action library of best practices for corporate entities and the legislation the nonprofit has helped draft in the process. Vantage anticipates a move to solar power for their embroidery machines based on the findings Clean Ocean Action was able to offer as the result of their audit.

ALLMADE - RYAN MOOR

A self-proclaimed graduate of the University of Rock and Roll, Ryan Moor turned his back on junior college and kicked off his music career, fueling his punk rock band with T-shirt and merchandise sales at their shows. This DIY spirit took hold with other bands who sought Ryan's expertise to do the same, and a marketplace was born.

In 2004, Ryan's e-commerce site silkscreeningsupplies.com took off, and the rest was history. Ryan has used a give-first strategy to build his business and his company. Ryonet is to this day an industry titan with more than 125,000 new screenprinting businesses started as a result of their efforts. Their supply chain touches more than 500 million shirts, a massive part of the overall US decorated apparel supply chain.

In growing from 0 to $8,000,000 in sales in 18 months, Ryan stood at the intersection of possibility and opportunity. As Ryan's role in the supply chain for T-shirts has grown, he's seen the apparel industry from a behind-the-scenes perspective. It was his reaction to what he saw that motivated him to action.

Ryan knew he had the opportunity to add a great T-shirt into his supply chain, and if done well, the product would have the possibility to be seen (and bought) by more buyers than in any other marketplace where those businesses supply their own production efforts. His desire to produce a high-quality product and the time, expense, and effort necessary to make that product come to life were consistently the obstacles to moving the process forward.

A chance introduction at the 2016 ISS Long Beach trade show led Ryan to the discovery of the Global Orphan Project.

In Haiti, 80 percent of orphans are not the result of death, rather they are the result of poverty. Unable to feed their children, Haitian parents were abandoning their children to orphanages. As many as 800,000 young people were abandoned. Due to the numbers of these economic orphans, the system was spiraling out of control. More displaced youth filled seats and beds as fast as they could be funded.

To counter this problem, Kansas City-based Global Orphan Project opened a business to employ these youth, pay them a living wage, and provide them training and support to help them maintain living-wage jobs as they age out of the system. The job? An apparel factory to make T-shirts.

Within 12 months, Allmade was born.

In late 2016, Ryan and a contingent of screenprint business owners descended on Haiti intent on building a brand around the project. Twenty-six people representing 12 screenprint decoration companies worked collaboratively to hammer out every element of the brand, from product construction and operations processes to the way the product would be marketed. Because of the sheer volume of products produced at each of these businesses, they knew they had the volume necessary to launch a product within the walls of their collective companies.

During the process, one of the stakeholders expressed a foundational desire to have the product leave the least damaging environmental impact possible. By moving away from polyester to alternative and recycled fibers, the group recognized an opportunity to capitalize on the added environmental impact this new product might realize, even at the expense of a more desirable price point.

The results have been extraordinary. In releasing the line to the open market, Allmade has sold more than 2 million pieces, and the following environmental impacts have occurred as a result:

490,000,000 gallons of water diverted from manufacturing use
95,000 pounds of chemicals not used in production
143,000 pounds of oil (63 drums) avoided
6,000,000 water bottles diverted from landfills
10,000 job days created
500 lives affected

Said Ryan:

> Many people think religion and the church will change the world, but it's really business that will change the world. Nonprofits, churches, they do great things, but there's not enough money in the world to be donated to solve the problems that we face, environmentally AND socially. We have to create change through commerce that creates a sustainable revenue source that can have an actual impact. The choices we make about what we buy and what we sell can ultimately make the difference we seek.

A partnership with Sanmar in 2020 brought was a total game-changer for the Allmade brand. As the largest apparel provider in the marketplace with 2019 revenues in excess of two billion dollars, the partnership with Sanmar brings mass appeal to the Allmade line. Expectations for sales and production are ambitious as the new partnership activated additional expansion of the manufacture of the product to Honduras and India. There was an accompanying expansion of the product line to include new fabrics and construction options given the expanded geography of the program.

In this time of pandemic, Allmade included the production of light-weight reusable and washable masks to their manufacturing line. Allmade pledged to donate a 3-pack of masks for every ten 3-packs sold via their website. To date they have been able to donate over 2,000 masks to those not able to purchase a mask for themselves.

To foster and encourage the community to join in the effort, Allmade created an online leaderboard and reported weekly masks-sold statistics from their Top 10 participants. Once the contest period ended, each Top 10 seller was given quantities of masks to donate to the recipient of their choice. First place received 1,000 masks. Second through fifth received 500 masks apiece, and sixth through tenth received 300 masks each for a grand total of 5,000 masks donated!

As a founding member of the Allmade collective, Denver-based screenprinter Dominic Rosacci said it best:

> When people make a conscious effort to create change, beautiful things can happen. When businesses decide to create change, **movements** happen.

REFRESH GLASS

Ray DelMuro abandoned a lucrative post-college career as a high-ranking engineer for Toyota in a quest to find more meaning for his work. The result? A quest to save 10 million wine bottles from destruction.

In what may have seemed an illogical move at the time, Ray cast aside his career of increasing responsibility and salary and traveled the world, visiting 21 countries and 39 cities in one calendar year. The objective? Finding a way to combine Ray's love for making things with a business model that could make a tangible difference in making the world a better place.

In Ray's manufacturing process, glass from Phoenix area establishments is saved and picked up by Refresh Glass employees and returned to their production facility where employees take the bottles through a process that reimagines the glass into Refresh drinking vessels, bottles, candle holders, and more.

Glass is an especially bad item for recycling companies. Because of the quantity and variability of components in the average glass bottle (label, cork, etc.), it's time-consuming and expensive to recycle. As a result, glass is often destroyed and added to the dirt in landfills, even if it gets to the recycling facility.

Consumers have taken notice. Refresh Glass products are featured prominently at iconic establishments like Spago at Caesar's Palace in Las Vegas, Husk in Charleston, and hundreds of restaurants and hospitality establishments around the world.

Buyers of Refresh Glass are rewarded twice, as the high quality and long-lasting products often are shared when in the presence of friends. By bringing out the product in the presence of guests, the owner has an opportunity to share the story behind the product, which often provides a positive mental correlation to Refresh Glass with those who hear the story.

Forbes and MSNBC have all featured Refresh Glass as a standard-bearer in the for-profit, for-purpose category.

While the journey to 10 million wine bottles saved has had moments of extreme success and occasional setbacks, it was the 2019 partnership with Waste Management for The Phoenix Open PGA event that really catapulted Refresh Glass to a new level. Their project with Waste Management as the signature sponsor of the event was the crowning achievement in showing a buyer of promotional marketing items how to incorporate what would otherwise have been waste into beautiful keepsakes commemorating the event. Keepsakes were subsequently distributed to attendees of the Waste Management Sustainability Forum. This shining example of closed-loop recycling, where products are used in their initial designation and then repurposed into additional uses, highlights a unique opportunity for buyers of branded products to consider ways to work additional uses into (and out of) the products their business is consuming.

Instead of viewing this event as a pinnacle, however, Ray sees it as the very beginning. As a "Made in the USA" product, Ray recognizes that the recent global health threat combined with trade restrictions with Chinese partners should increase interest in products made closer to home and believes that products with a story of philanthropy attached will only continue to grow in popularity with buyers as they start to make purchases again on behalf of their businesses. He says:

> This is a head, heart and soul buying decision. The head part of it is that it's a logical choice. It's dishwasher safe, it'll be around long enough to someday give it to your kids. The heart part is the emotion of knowing you're doing something good for the world. They're super stylish, take it from Francis Ford Coppola's Winery or Wolfgang Puck restaurants. The soul part is that we are actually moving the needle in the recycling world. We're walking the walk, too, we give products away to the local Habitat for Humanity. We're doing things like that every day.

It will be interesting to watch Refresh Glass continue to develop as a for-profit, for-purpose enterprise.

MEDIA TREE

Media Tree is a digital promotional marketing agency that specializes in providing entertainment rewards for gifting and incentive programs. Founded in 2005, MediaTree enjoyed early success in bringing digital music downloads to the Promotional Marketing industry and never looked back. (Thanks, iPod!)

Their products are redeemed online using an opt-in platform created to deliver a positive experience for the recipient. By utilizing the flexibility of e-gift codes, Media Tree delivers products and services across a broad range of categories, targeting numerous and varied age demographics at a variety of price points. Because of the nature of the program, very little physical product is produced. On top of that, redemption cards are flat and can be mailed physically if necessary, but the freight required to move these products is almost zero, a major incentive for buyers looking for an environmentally friendly way to build a positive brand image in the minds of the sustainability-minded.

Additionally, the rewards are pretty good. It's difficult to consistently deliver value across lower budget points, and items in the value category are most often made from the most environmentally damaging of products—plastic. Not all plastics are created equal, but the plastics found in the value category are often made from the most fragile of that substrate, which makes those items more prone to early breakage and a fast trip to the landfill.

MediaTree delivers a strong value for the money spent, and the gamut of choices available include movie rentals and tickets to the movie theater, eBook downloads, digital magazines, physical magazine subscriptions, even pizza, lunch, and a night out. It's hard not to find something you'd be happy to receive on someone else's dime, which is the intended result of any promotional marketing item.

The program is useful, interesting, and typically well-received by buyers. Many of those that ultimately purchase the program report high survey results when they ask recipients about receiving the product. The products receive a major score on the perceived value scale for any brand and provide one of the few instances of measurable ROI for a marketing investment, a long-held but rarely realized desire by corporate buyers. By introducing the digital platform, MediaTree realized an unintended benefit of being an incredibly strong eco-friendly product.

As MediaTree grew, they added developers and programmers. As the team grew, so did their desire to do something socially impactful. They realized an opportunity to be able to spin that collective desire into an opportunity to do something for the sake of social good. MediaTree leveraged the platform they'd created for good with the advent of their TreeCycler Program. Buyers purchase the program, and cards are distributed on behalf of the purchaser to recipients, who then redeem the gift by selecting where and for whom a tree will be planted. Participants are offered more than 40 reforestation projects all over the world as the destination for the tree planted in their honor.

Founder of MediaTree Bill Grassmyer said:

> One of the big things we witnessed in this program is the way participants flock to the social media pages of the company passing out the cards. The posts tend to be very personal, with stories about lost loved ones being shared by those for whom a tree was being planted. It often turns into something much more personal than anyone originally realized. We're giving people the chance to show they've done something even though it was someone else who made the investment.

The results have been impressive. Since its launch in 2012, Media-Tree has sold enough programs to equal *millions* of trees planted.

MediaTree recognizes the way the program has been utilized and made a realization that buyers of the program were reporting higher response rates compared to other forms of outreach. The program has been shown to be especially effective when used in conjunction with complementary environmental-based incentives, such as opting in for paperless billing.

A recent expansion of the program offers buyers a broader selection of giving categories, including the American Red Cross, Habitat for Humanity, H20 Trash Patrol, Feeding America, and more. By introducing additional choices, buyers are able to revisit the program for multiple applications, creating a unique opportunity for repeat and serial giving on the part of the buyer.

It's not lost on many practitioners in the Promotional Marketing industry that we have a responsibility to counter the potentially negative environmental consequences created when our product is used irresponsibly. Pictures of garbage cans overflowing with unwanted and discarded items at trade shows and conferences haunt us. The knowledge that a poorly executed promotional marketing campaign has a greater than likely chance of finding its way to the waste stream gives us pause, and for those of us willing to consider the way a poorly executed campaign adds to what is already a significant environmental challenge, we're driven to provide creativity to design and deliver campaigns that not only reverse that trend but create a corresponding positive environmental outcome instead.

By focusing our efforts on those businesses and products offering the opportunity to create a positive environmental outcome, promotional marketing consultants offer buyers a unique and emotionally-driven opportunity to align business values with personal ones. This is a growing trend as those buyers frequently appear as Millennials and Gen Zers—buyers already predisposed to making purchases based on corporate values as much as price.

These same buyer demographics are drawn to experiences. Their intense desire to document their lives creates built-in desires to attend and participate in memorable experiences that will populate their Instagram feeds with images of these memory-inducing moments. By engineering opportunities to create this type of memorable experience, businesses open the door to opportunities to interact with these high-value buyers, and by creating keepsakes and mementos, sellers create an opportunity to register a positive mental correlation in buyers' minds for their brand.

Promotional marketing experts thrive in the experience category. In the next chapter, we examine some of the most memorable events produced by members of this marketplace and the creative and thoughtful ways promotional marketing items are used to adeptly drive home the intended messages and emotions sellers attempt to convey to and elicit from buyers during these events.

CHAPTER 10

EXPERIENCE

"We don't remember days, we remember moments."

— Cesare Pavese

I've long asserted that the real power in our medium is not in the message it delivers, but the way it can make its recipients feel. This is the most important part of marketing. We also have the opportunity to make what we do extremely personal and create a memorable experience for the recipient.

Because promotional marketing items are most often exchanged in a person-to-person interaction, our medium is most frequently present in those instances where buyers and sellers meet. As a result, people dedicated to the industry are excellent at creating experiences, as it is in those experiences that our product is most often distributed. By virtue of our seemingly endless participation in all things experiential, promotional marketers have developed a cottage industry of marrying positive memories to branded items while combining an element of purpose in the mix. Ours is the only marketing medium recipients thank you for, and by combining elements of purpose into experiential marketing activations, brands create the opportunity for a longer-lasting impression than what's created in other forms of advertising.

To lift up and recognize the extraordinary efforts of many in our industry to make their communities a better place, Danny Rosin and I (Roger) co-founded PromoCares in late 2017. In the years that have ensued, we've welcomed additional industry members to the roster of volunteer leaders, so it now reads more like a who's who of purpose-driven experiential marketers in the Promotional Marketing industry. We're inspired by and in awe of the amazing events each of these business owners creates, and we've been lucky to participate in some incredible and life-changing experiences as a result of their hard work and dedication to the idea that doing good things is the best way to stand out.

We *are* the memorable events people. Our industry takes pride in dreaming up and executing big events that create lasting memories. Our people include the traveling trade show industry. The global health threat of 2020 imparted a tremendous toll on the events these big-hearted souls put on. The same has happened with in-person events. Our industry in many ways ground to a halt in the Spring of 2020, and it's an uncertain future for many practitioners in our space.

Prior to that, we had polished our philanthropy into some of the most memorable events and experiences available at the time. Pro-moCares board members gave away a TON of money to a bunch of really deserving people. Danny and the others covered in this chapter truly embody the ethos of using their businesses as super-powers for social good, the original mission of PromoCares and a foundational pillar of our effort to show the way forward for those interested in aligning on purpose. Here are their stories and the ways each of them are making their contributions noticed.

Danny Rosin - BandTogetherNC + Drum Team Collective™

Danny Rosin is a pathological optimist. He is a tireless connector focused on social innovation and fueling the power of marketing. With over 25 years of experience in philanthropy and marketing, he is focused on developing teams to help brands realize higher aspirations that will have a positive and sustainable impact on for-profit and nonprofit organizations.

With his 30+ year friend and business partner, Robert Fiveash, he is deeply invested in growing Reciprocity Road, a $220MM distributor-supplier partnership that crisscrosses the United States and Canada, with a strong corporate social responsibility initiative called "BrandGood."

Outside of Brand Fuel, Danny is the active co-founder of Band To-gether, a volunteer-driven organization that has donated over $10 million to 19 nonprofits through the Southeast's largest charitable concert event. This once-yearly love fest that fills downtown Ra-leigh's Red Hat Amphitheater with full hearts and eventually empty pockets as supporters of the organization flock to the event from all over the country to raise money for a different and worthy Triangle-area nonprofit each year.

The model, dubbed Partnership Philanthropy, is unique in that the nonprofit beneficiary receives not only the financial contribution (which most years flirts with or surpasses one million dollars given) but also support from BandTogetherNC in the form of leadership, direction, and guidance. Thanks to the tireless efforts of thousands of volunteers, generous corporate and individual sponsors, dedicated board members, musicians, and the generosity of the community, Band Together has risen to be a powerful partner for nonprofits in the Triangle Area.

Promotional marketing items adorn the event. Wristbands, T-shirts, signage, sunglasses, and more all become key elements in the festival atmosphere of the show. Volunteers are all given a matching tee, and social media is splashed each year with photos of massive legions of big-hearted participants rocking their tees in the annual volunteer wrap-up photo.

As the global health threat descended in 2020, BandTogetherNC was forced to cancel what would have been their 20th anniversary event, intended to honor the more than 1,500 people and the legions of businesses who have lent a hand to the show and the multitude of regional, national, and international artists who've shared an evening with concertgoers in the name of raising funds for a worthy cause. As a result of the cancellation, branded merchandise has taken on even greater importance. The organization launched a full-blown merchandise campaign complete with an opportunity for the purchaser of their products to suggest the nonprofit for which the proceeds of their purchase would be designated.

Danny didn't let a global health threat alter his approach to using promotional marketing as a memorable experience. If anything, he doubled down, launching Drum Team Collective with professional musician Mike McKee of the band Delta Rae. Drum Team Collective is a unique team-building experience where participants are taught the elements of being a drummer in a band.

Dubbed "Rock and Roll Team Building," these 90-minute experiences promote bonding and team building while working together to create drum grooves. Participants are left raving after the event, claiming empowerment and fun as the most frequent takeaways.

Drum sets are separated into "stations" for each participant. A Drum Team Collective instructor explains the role of each instrument and how to play it. The group then plays drum patterns together, and a live house band joins in to play well-known songs along with the team.

Again, promotional marketing items play an important role. Participants receive branded drum sticks, Bluetooth speakers, wireless earphones/earbuds, journals made out of recycled albums, bottle openers made out of recycled albums, and rock-style T-shirts.

Mandi Rudd/David Shultz - BigSlick KC

Commonsku VP of Supplier Partnerships David Shultz is a member of the Big Slick Organizers Community and is involved in everything from running digital marketing for the entire event to managing the weekend karaoke competition.

Mandi Rudd is the sister of comedian Paul Rudd, Big Slick's host and co-founder, and is a key member of the family of volunteers at Big Slick. She is also the owner of Brand Energy Marketing, a firm that specializes in marketing strategies and promotional products.

Big Slick rang in its tenth year as a charity event in 2019, having now raised more than $10 million dollars in total for the Pediatric Cancer Center at Kansas City Children's Mercy Hospital.

What started as a poker tournament that raised $150,000 has grown into a weekend packed full of events, garnering well-known celebrity talent participation from the acting, music, and comedy worlds, including David Koechner, Rob Riggle, Eric Stonestreet, and Jason Sudeikis. Dubbed "Hilarity for Charity," the 2019 event saw more than 30 celebrity participants.

The events are fast and furious. Tickets to a celebrity softball game prior to a Kansas City Royals game also qualifies as tickets for the Royals game that night. There's a street fair, a block party, and a bowling tournament. Capping the event, there is a celebrity red carpet walk for kids from the hospital and their parents, finished off with a concert in the largest venue in town.

Promotional marketing takes a front seat in the fundraising process. T-shirts, cups, and all forms of swag sold create additional revenue streams to augment efforts by sponsors and donors to raise funds before, during, and after the event.

Strong emotional ties to the event and its objective caught the eye of iconic Kansas City based apparel designer Charlie Hustle.

David Shultz of commonsku says:

> A promotional product has become a very large part of what we do in terms of off-line fundraising before the event. We have a lot of merchandise . . . t-shirts, hats, all those kinds of things that we sell over the course of the weekend. But we wanted one thing that someone could buy that showed they were a donor of a certain level for Big Slick. So, we took the NPR approach, when you donate $20 you get your NPR coffee mug and everyone gets to see that you're a supporter.
>
> We took the same approach and had a local designer in Kansas City design a tee shirt for us that we could

use to recognize donors at the $100 level to be able to get this limited-edition piece. This is year 6 we've done this and that silly little [tee] shirt has been a part of our fundraising every year—we average close to $100,000 each year from the sale of these tees. People participate each and every year in the program and they've become collector's items to a certain degree.

Hundreds of thousands of dollars spent on promotional items are hard to deny. By creating an emotional connection to the cause, Big Slick has created commemorative pieces that are sought after, highly desirable, and an overt symbol of personal participation in a growing effort to support causes.

As with BandTogetherNC, Big Slick was unfortunately forced to cancel its 2020 event. To help offset some of the lost revenue from the cancellation of the event, Big Slick organizers turned to the power of promotional marketing, partnering again with Charlie Hustle to create and sell online commemorative "Kegger at My Mom's House" T-shirts to coincide with the victory celebration that followed the NFL's Kansas City Chiefs 2020 Super Bowl win. These limited-edition $50 tees netted Children's Mercy $25 for each shirt sold and generated $10,000 in donations.

One of many negative effects caused by the global health threat is the absence of critical in-person fundraising events for nonprofits who count heavily on them as a vital economic engine for the communities they serve. As these nonprofits scramble to create and implement new and interesting ways for the donor community to support them, it's important for each of us in our industry to consider how we as supporters of their work might also find new and interesting ways to offer our support from a time, talent, and treasure perspective.

Sarah White & Denise Taschereau - Soccer League for the Homeless

One of the precious few certified B Corporations in the Promotional Marketing industry, Fairware Promotional Products' stated mission is to change the world through the simple act of buying. They are change-makers who have made sustainability, ethical sourcing, and inclusive hiring practices the legs of their stool from the outset of their business in 2005, and their company is looked to by many in the Promotional Marketing industry as the North Star of purpose-driven behaviors. It was Denise's addition to the PromoCares Board of Directors in 2020 that fueled an effort to sharpen the PromoCares mission and evolve its ability to serve as stewards of purpose-driven behaviors for others in the marketplace.

Fairware for years has supported a local organization called the Vancouver Street Soccer League (VSSL), a volunteer-run organization dedicated to area homelessness, those marginalized within their communities, or those recovering from drug and alcohol addictions. The organization relies entirely on donations to execute on its mission.

The VSSL addresses its players' needs through inclusivity and soccer, believing they can enhance all lives through the principles of Fair Play, Community Building, Supportive Partnerships, and Health and Safety.

Fairware began by donating sample apparel and goods and supplying printed apparel at deep discounts. In 2013, they donated uniforms for all players in the organization and co-founder Sarah White joined the newly created board to help build capacity and raise much-needed funds. She was subsequently joined by two additional members of the company, who saw Sarah's efforts and offered to participate.

Every year, the 'Namgis First Nation hosts an invitation-only soccer tournament during Father's Day weekend. In 2019, close to 40 players and volunteers from the VSSL headed to Alert Bay, British Columbia, to participate. The village parade and traditional long-house ceremonies that kick off the tournament resonate deeply with many of the players, particularly those who rarely leave the Downtown Eastside neighborhood. For those players struggling with mental illness or living in shelters, the long trip up-island, natural beauty of Alert Bay, and scenic boat rides can be particularly refreshing and rejuvenating. The camaraderie forged on the soccer field or at the camping site while dining over communal meals after a hard-fought match makes this trip a highlight of the year.

Fairware also hires players from the street soccer league to work at Fairware to assist with their packing and shipping efforts. Plus Fairware hosts an annual "Holiday Haul" where community members, Fairware's clients, and other donors interested in supporting the league bring gifts for the players and their kids and good old cash to pay for food, equipment, and tournament fees in the coming year. Denise says, *"Business has incredible power to drive positive change. For us, sustainability isn't a sidebar—it's our mission."*

Karie Cowden - World Record Flip-Flop Race for Charity

Founded on April Fool's Day 2008 in Arizona, Phoenix-based and WBENC-certified Connect the Dots Promotions is the brainchild of PromoCares Board Member Karie Cowden. By day, Karie's company works with clients to create experiences around their brand using promotional marketing items focusing on sustainability and safety. In addition to being a mom and a wife along with her business role, Karie serves as the host of the PromoCares Radio podcast, where she speaks with members of the Promotional Marketing industry and documents the ways buyers and sellers in our industry are adopting a purpose-driven organizational strategy. Karie's podcasts have generated thousands of listens, and her continued efforts to tell those stories keeps the PromoCares brand top of mind with buyers and sellers in our space. More importantly, it creates opportunities for the ultimate final buyers of our products to learn more about the ways their purchases of branded merchandise might benefit the world in a positive way through the stories documented there.

She's also a Guinness World Record holder. In 2018, Karie and her team chaired the committee that produced what became a Guinness World Record winning thong sandal race. These 1Ks are produced as fundraisers for United Methodist Outreach Ministries, an organization dedicated to Phoenix-area residents at risk of homelessness and abuse.

In 2019 for the 11th annual edition of the race, 1,942 big-hearted thong sandal enthusiasts raced, raising nearly $150,000 for the ministry to serve the needs of the community. All registrations included a T-shirt and flip-flops in addition to an all-day, same-day pass to the Phoenix Zoo. Due to Karie's willingness to inject some new ideas into what had become stagnant fundraising, UMOM was able to realize a 67 percent increase in donations as a result of adding the Guinness World Record angle.

Every night, more than 150 families experience homelessness in Maricopa County, waiting to escape the unsafe environment of living on the streets, sleeping in their cars, or residing in an unstable living situation. Families may wait more than six weeks before a shelter unit is available. UMOM's goal is to eliminate shelter waiting lists and help each family, single woman, or young person as they need it. Karie's dedication and willingness to assume greater responsibility for the marketing of the event coupled with her courage to take on the existing Guinness record holder and a desire to motivate the necessary number of racers to win the record makes her a stellar example for promotional marketing consultants providing greater value than purchasing product from an internet search engine or on Amazon. com. She delivered on her company mission to create an experience. Karie said, "If you call me and ask me to buy something, my first question will be to ask why you want to make that choice. I believe we're not "trinkets and trash" and landfill. We should be doing more and elevating [our] industry, too."

I (Roger) am often quoted as saying, "If you hang around with inspirational people long enough, you'll eventually be inspired. It's like it's osmosis." By surrounding myself with this group of motivated, inspirational people intent on getting shit done and by documenting the stories of the companies in our marketplace using their business to benefit their community and the causes they care so much about, I discovered the inspiration to found my own business, Social Good Promotions, in 2019. I'm grateful for and energized by their stories as told in this section and look forward to the opportunity to achieve the same level of community contribution as those I'm repeatedly surrounded by. Hopefully, the stories of this group's achievements in creating memorable, life-changing events will serve as a measure of inspiration to use your own talent to create something similar. Stick around in these pages long enough and you just might find the osmosis I'm talking about.

While you seek your own inspiration, let's consider the exploding importance of trust and transparency in the relationship between consumers and brands.

CHAPTER 11

TRANSPARENCY & TRUST

*"People don't trust companies, brands and advertisers.
They trust one another."*

— Mark W. Schaefer

As mentioned previously in the book, Sanmar is seen by many as the best example in the Promotional Marketing industry of a business leading via transparency and demonstrating a willingness to report on their efforts in a manner suitable for other businesses in the industry to follow.

Family-owned and operated since 1971, SanMar, based in Issaquah, Washington, has grown to the point where it now vies annually for the status of largest Supplier by revenue in the industry and boasted near 50 percent growth in 2019, becoming the first supplier in the industry to top $2 Billion in annual sales, regaining the #1 spot on the 2020 list from industry conglomerate alphabroder. Employing more than 4,000 people across eight United States distribution centers, SanMar also employs apparel manufacturers from such far-away places as Central America, Africa, India, and Asia.

The most obvious example of this leadership approach to Corporate Social Responsibility takes shape in Sanmar's Corporate Responsibility Report. Originally published in 2018 to reflect their corporate efforts from 2014 – 2017 and due for a major update in early 2021 to reflect the period from 2018 forward, the report represents SanMar's attempt to report on the key metrics they've identified as being important to their Organizational mission and objectives.

In his letter to open the most recent report, Company president and second generation leader Jeremy Lott outlined agree the ways these efforts have intertwined themselves into SanMar company culture:

> When we first began outlining our approach to corporate responsibility, we realized that much of what it means to be a responsible business is already woven into our SanMar Family Values. Today we are more passionate than ever about living our values by supporting our communities, delivering sustainable products and taking action to reduce our environmental

impact. We are still charting our corporate responsibility efforts and know there is much work ahead. We are committed to continuing to make thoughtful choices and a positive impact.

These SanMar Family Values and the way they're tied to CSR is explained below in greater detail:

Our commitment to corporate responsibility combines all of our SanMar Family Values, driving us to support the people who create, ship and sell our apparel and accessories; to deliver quality, sustainable products that are ethically and responsibly sourced; and to do the right thing for our planet.

In a 2018 interview, Jeremy offered the following:

"We realized over time that we wanted to evolve away from a thought process that was governed by the idea of not doing bad things and toward a new process that had us consider "How do we do POSITIVE things for the communities we're active in, and how can we collectively make the world a better place in that context."

The company believes so strongly in the concept that the idea has become not only a foundational pillar of company culture, but also an organizational rallying cry as many SanMar employees are on record as saying it was the CSR-based philosophy that attracted them to the company and a big reason why most employees stay for years.

The Report is organized into three categories: People, Product, and Planet, and within each of those sections, SanMar reports the metrics they've compiled in each category—statistics that serve as benchmarks for the company against their desired performance in each area. What's noteworthy is those areas where the Company reports less-than-desired results and their plan to fix what didn't work in that category. In the most recent report, for example, San-Mar reported an 8 percent increase in water consumption and a corresponding dedication to adhering more closely to the Higg index to reverse this trend. Developed by the Sustainable Apparel Coalition, the Higg Index is a suite of tools that enables brands, retailers, and facilities of all sizes—at every stage in their sustainability journey—to accurately measure and score a company or product's sustainability performance. The Higg Index delivers a holistic overview that empowers businesses to make meaningful improvements that protect the well-being of factory workers, local communities, and the environment.

SanMar announced their partnership with the AllMade brand in early 2020. This partnership will expand the volume of AllMade products available to purchasers of decorated apparel, and this relationship is sure to mean greater reach for the AllMade brand, as SanMar boasts a client roster of over 60,000 unique businesses. By making the AllMade brand a more viable alternative for a larger roster of potential buyers, they are remaining true to their aspirational goals for 2020 as outlined in the 2018 report, which included categories devoted to Women and Children & Sustainable Products among others.

It's hard to be certain if SanMar's strategic commitment to Corporate Social Responsibility is the key differentiating factor when one points to their industry-leading sales performance, but Jeremy himself suggested in a recent interview that their family values and a focus on making a difference in the community was their chief go-to-market strategy for future generations of the company.

"LIFE IS TOO SHORT TO NOT BE NICE,"

Mark Schaefer is one of the most widely known marketing writers working today. In his book *Marketing Rebellion*, Mark outlines his perspectives on the how and why consumers have wrestled responsibility for marketing from the brands with which they associate themselves.

He put the position bluntly:

> Reports by numerous research firms have asserted that loyalty is over, the sales funnel is over. People are in control of their own journey. Not only that, the customers are in charge of our marketing. The customers ARE the marketers.

If, as Mark asserts, nearly two-thirds of your brand's marketing activities are being done independent of any investment you've made in growing your reach, how can brands better align themselves with the efforts happening away from them?

Quick Answer: It requires an invitation from the community to be a part of those efforts.

Based on the principles presented in *Marketing Rebellion*, Mark suggests anything beyond waiting for (and graciously accepting) that invitation will be seen as an intrusion—and the worst thing any brand can do today is to be seen as intrusive or manipulative in an attempt to be accepted by "your people."

In addition to the evidence presented brilliantly in Mark's book, signs of growing distrust by the average American in traditionally trusted sources for change in the country have been met with equally growing signs of these same Americans frequently looking toward their employer to replace those trust-based institutions.

Consider the following statistics and analysis from the 2019 Edelman Trust Barometer.

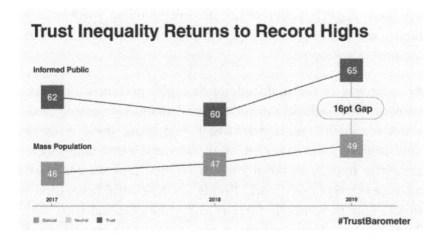

Trust Inequality Returns to Record Highs

Informed Public

62 · 60 · 65

16pt Gap

Mass Population

46 · 47 · 49

2017 · 2018 · 2019

Distrust · Neutral · Trust

#TrustBarometer

Divided by Trust

There is a 16-point gap between the more trusting informed public and the far-more-skeptical mass population, marking a return to record highs of trust inequality. The phenomenon fueling this divide was a pronounced rise in trust among the informed public. Markets such as the US, UK, Canada, South Korea, and Hong Kong saw trust gains of 12 points or more among the informed public. In 18 markets, there is now a double-digit trust gap between the informed public and the mass population.

An Urgent Desire for Change

Despite the divergence in trust between the informed public and mass population, the world is united on one front—all share an urgent desire for change. Only one in five feels that the system is working for them, with nearly half of the mass population believing that the system is failing them. In conjunction with pessimism and worry, there is a growing move toward engagement and action. In 2019, engagement with the news surged by 22 points; 40 percent not only consume news once a week or more but they also routinely amplify it. But people are encountering roadblocks in their quest for facts, with 73 percent worried about fake news being used as a weapon.

Be it by way of the multitude of examples presented in Mark's book or the insightful information and analysis presented in the always excellent report produced by Edelman, these resources only solidify what many of us in sales and marketing already recognize by way of the numerous relationships we create and nurture as part of our work. People are distrustful beyond those they're able to routinely interact and grow personal trust with. The global pandemic and the resultant rancor it's created is only fanning the flames of distrust.

Many consumer brands were caught flat-footed on how to communicate their brand values as the pandemic took hold. As a result, most of them produced and distributed generic ads that did little more than serve as an advertising placeholder for the era. With a lack of clarity on their purpose, most organizations were rendered incapable of reacting in a genuine way that could connect with their most sought-after prospects. Worse, the homogenous nature of these placeholder ads quickly became fodder for those trolling for examples of dollars wasted on marketing messaging. This "lack of optics" on the part of advertisers was championed as an example of corporate waste, with the suggestion being that the dollars spent on those unimpressive, generic messages of support should have been traded for ACTUAL dollars in ACTUAL support for those ads intended audiences.

As the recovery of the economy finds its legs, expectations suggest an even greater increase in consumer desire to personally connect with businesses in their economy. Organizations aligned on purpose will be more capable of rapidly creating these personal connections as purpose itself is an emotional trigger for many, and purpose-based activities offer a universal appeal across all demographics and psychographics.

When Social Good Promotions was launched in early 2019, it was to meet purchasers where they need to be met—in the intersection of logic and emotion. People make buying decisions emotionally and use logic to justify their emotional decision. By aligning with partners with a defensible community impact strategy built into their business, buyers have the opportunity to connect the emotion they want to stir in others about *their* businesses. The solutions built by Social Good Promotions activates positive mental correlation between customers/client/donors and the businesses and/or non-profits wanting to serve them.

With 2019 as the first year in business in what has been and will continue to be a complicated tangle of geo-political, social, and health-related concerns, our annualized sales results outperformed a typical two-person sales operation by about 200 percent. This year, 2020, was off to a fast start as well until the economy was halted, and as of the time of this writing, the company is faced with a reopening economy and an arm's length list of requests from potential new clients.

Why was the company able to get out to a fast start in one of the hardest-hit markets in the country? Trust.

It's a universally held truth that people generally buy from people they know, like, and trust. This truth has become so pervasively held that many people don't consider its true meaning and the role this know/like/trust continuum plays in earning business success.

Many people equate the path from know to like to trust as being akin to downhill skiing—a dangerous adventure for many, fraught with peril and the possibility of injury and/or embarrassment in the process. When the average person considers a role in sales, it's often this mental image that stands in their way, and for those already employed in sales roles, it's this concept of that fearful journey that often stands in the way of top-level performance. If it's necessary to face mountains of rejection, why bother trying?

If that sounds familiar, consider the following.

What if the journey to trust was more like climbing to the top of an Egyptian pyramid? How would that change your thought process? If committing to the process of climbing to the top required a dedicated effort to developing the skills needed to make the climb, would you put in the effort? If, on that climb, you realized the path you'd been on had suddenly become untenable, would you be willing to sidestep your current route to continue your climb? In short, can you commit to the repeated activities necessary to get to that spot in your clients' hearts that ensures you will be the person they reach out to in their time of need?

When COVID-19 overtook the state of Michigan, the economy ground to a halt. In that "time in pause," only the most trusted partners were those that any of us chose to spend time with. In many instances, business owners offered their services for free to others in their trusted circles in the hope that those positive contributions might someday benefit the relationship. The results were often remarkable.

Attempts to sell outside of those circles of trust in that period (a period that may have yet to end) were often met with objection and, in many instances, those attempts were met with hostility. Seemingly feeble and poorly executed sales efforts were no longer looked upon as mere "stubs of the proverbial toe." They were black eyes that in some instances left an indelible mark that a company may not be able to recover from.

While attempts at sales outside of the top of the know/like/trust pyramid might be met with hostility, that doesn't mean that businesses should cease their attempts to connect with their potential

TRUST INDEX

Understanding and planning for varying degrees of trust in your clients and prospects allows you to see your relationships from new perspectives.

OHANA

What difference might we make?
Who can benefit from our collaboration?
What problem can we solve together?

STRONG

Where can we go together?
What would make you a superhero?
Who can make our team better?

NEUTRAL

What are you passionate about?
Where are you most comfortable?
How do we connect more deeply?

WEAK

Where are our common interests?
What answers are you seeking?
How are you surviving and thriving?

NEGATIVE

Negative feedback, bad reviews, and poor ratings are often the result of organizational failures - quarterly post-mortems and a willingness to improve are required.

BEGIN EACH NEW ENCOUNTER WITH TRUST IN MIND.

client base. What it DOES mean, however, is there must be a mind-set change on the part of salespeople to recognize the increased meaning of trust in this new normal as well as a determination whether sales activities are in line with where you are in the "trust continuum."

By approaching each new encounter with a healthy eye toward the status of your trust relationship with those you're interacting with, you give yourself the best chance possible to develop credibility and authority in the mind of those with whom you're interacting. By adopting a trust-centered position, you create better opportunities to serve the relationship you're seeking to develop.

Let's examine each of the categories to better understand the activities that are most suitable for each phase in the continuum.

We begin with a look at NEGATIVE TRUST RELATIONSHIPS: Relationships are like quicksand. You can find yourself with a bad review, a negative comment, or a misinterpreted social media post. No matter where you are on your climb to Trust, the possibility of a fall into a negative relationship is always lurking. While many choose to turn a blind eye to those instances when others prove to be less than raving fans, it's vitally important to have a strategy to deal with negative situations. It is often your response to and the way you handle these situations that will create loyal fans. In many instances, fans and followers of your brand will defend you against negative attacks if you've built brand loyalty, so ignoring your weaknesses can work against you.

WEAK TRUST RELATIONSHIPS: It's safe to assume that most relationships you'll begin start in a weak position. It's relatively un-likely that someone will bother to give you their time if they already have a negative opinion of you, and it's just as unlikely that most people will have done enough homework to have a stronger than neutral trust position, especially in B2B sales. In weak trust relationships, the person at least knows who you are but not much else.

You most likely are not yet certain yourself that this person will meet your criteria for being a client, so by focusing your activities on trust in this moment, you improve the opportunity to shorten the amount of time necessary to decide if you should invest in developing the relationship further.

NEUTRAL TRUST RELATIONSHIPS: Neutral relationships often develop through a combination of active and passive interactions with your brand. Maybe they've seen something on social media that caught their attention. Maybe they've seen you comment and interact with other people that they're connected to. They're starting to get a sense of what you're all about, but they're still relatively uninvested in moving you ahead in their heads and hearts. Behaviors in neutral trust relationships should be focused on creating opportunities to bring an increasingly more personal level of value to your interactions.

It's usually in the transition from Neutral to Strong relationships that transactions begin to occur. By deciding to give you a shot, your customer is validating your effort to build a relationship with them by being willing to spend some of their resources with you, be that time, talent, or money.

STRONG TRUST RELATIONSHIPS: In strong relationships, you've developed a rapport that gives you the opportunity to bring truly crafted solutions to the table. In these relationships, you're given insights that serve as keys to your collective success and those who trust you will often share exclusive pieces of information that can make the difference between someone people buy from and someone people rely on to succeed.

OHANA: The word ohana means family in the Hawaiian language, but in a much wider sense to include not only closer relatives but also cousins, in-laws, friends, and other neighbors. The idea is also that family and friends are bound together and everyone must work together and not forget each other. Once you've achieved ohana status, you've become a member of their family. A wide range of customers, suppliers, service providers, nonprofits, and peers of ours in the Promotional Marketing industry are our ohana. Our community has supported us in countless ways during this memorable time in American history, and it is largely because of our focus on purpose that people have rallied to our aid.

By focusing on building increasing levels of trust during the Shelter in Place order, Social Good Promotions was able to organize our activities and focus our attention on creating ways to educate, inform, entertain, and inspire people. With most people having more time on their hands than at any other time in modern society, we doubled down on our efforts to provide high-quality, long-form content that focused on the inspirational stories behind the efforts of our soGOOD Supply Co. partners. We spent countless hours sharing those stories with anyone willing to take the time to watch.[16]

When you're working on improving trust and seeking to communicate that which makes you unique, it's incredibly important to try and create an emotional connection with your prospects. This is what we did with the soGOOD interviews. Success in accomplishing this task will solidify your position as a brand and will stick in the minds of buyers. They'll tell their friends about your brand and encourage them to buy what you sell as well. We call this "the Cyclone of Good."

By focusing on purpose and working diligently to tell the stories behind what happens when businesses choose to align with Social Good Promotions, the company has been a sought-after choice to solve unique problems clients have brought to the table. It's clear

---

16. https://socialgoodpromotions.com/sogood-supply-co/

that the ability to improve the perception of the company was driven largely by the ability to provide unique value to the community when they were in their hour of need. Social Good Promotions lived its brand when times got tough, and it was that commitment that's been rewarded as people re-engage in the business of doing business in a post- COVID-19 economy.

CREATING PURPOSE

CHAPTER 12

DEVELOPING A PURPOSE STATEMENT

"In the culture of Okinawa, ikigai is thought of as a reason to get up in the morning; that is, a reason to enjoy life. It is suggested as one of the reasons people in the area have such long lives."

— Dan Buettner, TEDx Talk

This part of the book is meant to serve two purposes:

1. For members of the Promotional Marketing industry, it's our sincere wish that you not only find this book informational but you also believe sharing the story with your customers, prospects, local high schools and colleges, and non-profits in your community will result in an improved impression of the Promotional Marketing industry. For too long too many people have minimized the value of a consultant in our space. I believe with an improved focus on delivering differentiated value, there is tremendous opportunity in combining purpose with commerce. I've made it my life's work to pursue this concept and this book is meant to serve as a guidemap for you on your own journey to developing a purpose statement for your own businesses.

2. For buyers of advertising, it's never been more important for you to be able to communicate. what it is that your prospective buyers should feel as a result of giving you their money. Can they feel confident that your efforts will support the narrative they've built for themselves? If you've not built this into your brand, you will suffer going forward against competition that's capable in that discipline. By aligning on purpose, you're giving yourself a proven advantage over those who choose other alternatives or no articulated strategy in this discipline.

Regardless of the category with which you most closely identify, the creation of your own purpose statement as outlined in the pages ahead would serve you well. In both these instances, the crafting of a purpose statement as articulated below. We've woven anecdotes from the Promotional Marketing industry into this part of the book, but you need not be a promotional marketing company to follow this strategy.

With that, let's consider how to bring this newfound desire of yours to life.

By this point in the book, hopefully you've come up with a few ideas on a purpose that might be a good fit for your organization. If you're like most business owners, regardless of the marketplace in which you compete, the task of formulating, developing, and implementing that purpose can seem a bit daunting. You may wonder how you can convince your organization to get on board and develop a business purpose that fits with your company culture, organizational structure, and competitive challenges.

In the course of the average workday, very few staffers will ever mention or ever think about their company's purpose and mission. The day-to-day tasks of driving revenue and keeping the operation humming take up most of our time and mental energy.

Most of us tend to rely on leaders to articulate the purpose of a business and then to build systems that bring that purpose to life. But managers typically are focused on the logistics of projects in the pipeline rather than whether those projects demonstrate the company's core purpose.

Some companies have clearly articulated their vision within their strategic documents while others never mention vision at all. There are many amazing purpose-driven companies that never sat down and created a purpose definition document. Typically they are blessed with leaders who intrinsically stay on purpose by following their own internal compass.

No question, having a written purpose statement is a huge asset in communicating a purpose, but it's not something you need to worry about in the beginning stages. You can get to that later. Right now, the important thing is that you start and follow that fire in your belly that brings more meaning to your work and the work done by everyone in the company.

GETTING STARTED

The beginning stages are all about formulating and then learning to articulate your vision. Before you can share your thoughts about your company's business purpose, the thoughts should be directed to something tangible, and they should be easily understood.

As you begin to formulate, it is important that you carefully consider the beliefs and attitudes of your coworkers. Most businesses tend to follow the traditional business model goals of Milton Friedman. They see their company as principally a **transactional** entity. Business purpose is primarily embodied in the things they produce, not in the Zeitgeist of the organization. Most believe that if the business is making money and clients are satisfied, the company is "on purpose." They feel that if they take care of the basics, the larger concerns like purpose are not really necessary.

Some will even see purpose discussions as an indulgent dalliance that could be a distraction from the primary goal—making money. Anyone who saunters into the boss's office and demands a purpose statement is probably going to be told to get back to work and refocus their priorities on the tasks at hand.

The best purpose statements are initiated and shepherded by top managers, but if your company managers have not articulated their vision does that mean you should browbeat them into it?

When developing an effective purpose statement, it is important to remember that the process is one of **evolution** and not **revolution**. In our training and consulting work we often see purpose statements that have been created in a vacuum by a well-meaning committee. Purpose statements created by sequestered groups are sometimes created solely for PR reasons. The purpose statement will appear boldly at the top of the annual report and in other public documents, then be shelved and never seen again.

These purpose statements can contain lofty, unattainable goals that have little to do with reality. Read through many company purpose statements and you'll find laudable goals that are, however, completely detached from the company's day-to-day operations. Purpose statements must embrace real-world conditions. They cannot ignore the pragmatic truths, momentum, phobias, and dysfunctions that are a part of any company. They cannot underestimate the major forces of company culture, financial realities, competitive pressures, and other important marketplace conditions.

Whatever purpose your company creates, it's important that you not delude yourself. Living a strong company purpose is going to be very hard work and will often require very hard choices being made. CVS stopped selling cigarettes because it conflicted with their purpose to help customers live healthier lives. That decision was a frightening one because it meant CVS would be eliminating a very profitable product line. Today, the company is glad it made that call, but at the time, it was hotly debated within the company.

STARTING CONVERSATIONS

The process of developing a company purpose statement should start small. It should begin with casual conversations around the water cooler. It should be an unpretentious, friendly conversation among coworkers. It could begin with an easygoing question to your supervisor.

Questions like, "What is the purpose of our entire organization?" can be somewhat daunting. We recommend that you make the language more approachable and that you focus on the day-to-day priorities of your company. A good question we like to use is "what's the good our company hopes to do for our customers, employees, and community?"

Realize that these conversations will take a bit of persistence. The first response you likely will get to the question above will have a **product-focused** response. "What good do we do?" will solicit a reply such as, "We produce or distribute fantastic products at a good price and deliver real value for our customers." While that's true, it's also what every company in the world hopes to do. That's not a description of your purpose, it's a description of your daily operational goals. It's a tactic, not a goal. That response doesn't adequately describe the consequences and outcomes of all that hard work your company does each day.

Be sure to follow up the product-focused response with "why do we do that?" Then keep asking "why" until that person reveals their larger vision of the company's overarching purpose.

A typical conversation might go something like this. Let's say you happen to own a business in the promotional products industry and you're presented with this set of questions from a prospect, or equally or perhaps even more importantly, a potential new hire.

THEY: "What's the good our company hopes to do for our customers, employees, and community?

US: "We want our customers and their brands to stand out from their competitors because of the work we do with them on aligning their beliefs with their go to market strategy."

THEY: "Why do we do that?"

US: "Because when they can communicate what it is their brands stand for and can show it in a meaningful way, they sell more, have happier employees, and can see a common path forward better than ever. They work harder and are far more dedicated when they understand the greater purpose of the company."

THEY: "What's the ultimate benefit of this approach?"

US: Happy employees make for noteworthy performance, but brands who find alignment enjoy results that outperform the marketplace in a way that is noteworthy to investors, both financial investors and motivated fans of your brand willing to share your efforts with their loved ones

THEY: "What I hear you saying is that the purpose of our company is to help people connect their brand with the things they really care about. Is that our company's purpose?"

What you will notice about this conversation is that we quickly took the conversation from a discussion of daily business tasks to a conversation about *the effects* of those tasks. Keep climbing up, one step at a time. Mirror the person's last response, putting a "why" in front of it. Use this "why" technique until you've gotten to a bigger place that is a description of an important priority that is key to your customer's vision of herself.

You'll know you've arrived when you are no longer talking about what your company manufactures and are discussing something that would really bring a smile to your stakeholder's face. Why? Because these desires are central to your stakeholder's life and would endure even if your product didn't exist. In the best instances, this improved relationship should be considered a triple win—a win for both the seller, the buyer, and their shared belief or cause that wins as a result of this new partnership.

IDENTIFYING YOUR COMPANY'S BENEFIT TO STAKEHOLDERS

The best purposes are pragmatic ones that are not so all-encompassing that they become unattainable. Stay away from "save the world" purposes that lack accountability. For example, turn the inaccessible purpose of "save the environment" to the more attainable purpose of "We help our stakeholders better understand how the products they buy affect the planet."

We would encourage you to give a lot of thought to how your company's customers, employees, and vendors feel about themselves *after* they've interacted with your company. What is the effect of your products and services on their lives? How has your company made a difference to them? Again, be sure that you ask that "why" over and over again to get to that greater purpose. If you find yourself describing benefits that are intrinsic to every competitor in the sector, you're probably still mired in the basics.

This is a pervasive concept in the Promotional Marketing industry. Ask most buyers of products in that marketplace where they source products from and you'll quickly realize most buyers want NO interaction with a salesperson to buy items adorned with their logo. Yet, when surveyed, those same buyers report poor results in the effectiveness of the producs they buy, a problem most easily solved by involving a promotional marketing consultant during the product sourcing process.

If you're struggling with ways to bring out those emotional outcomes you're looking for, promotional marketing campaigns designed with the help of consultants have a significant impact on the dollar-for-dollar effectiveness of those purchases, often the kind of effectiveness not easily found when navigating other digital marketing alternatives. The alternatives may be cheaper on a per-click basis, but a well-designed marketing campaign featuring a memorable piece of branded merchandise has proven time and again to be one of the best dollar-for-dollar investments when return on capital is calculated. Plus, they're things people hold on to forever when they're done well.

It's important that you puff up your chest a little and really dig into the transcendent effects your company brings to the world. Sure, for those of us in the daily grind of bringing a product to market, it's easy to lose touch with how that product actually influences lives. People pay you their hard-earned cash to buy that product and that product helps them achieve a goal in their life. If your product wasn't important in their lives, they'd stop buying it. Here are some examples from other industries:

- The best restaurants don't play the small game of just serving food. They see themselves as an important gathering place that builds family bonds. All restaurants are dedicated to a square meal at a good price. A purpose-driven restaurant might be dedicated to making *families stronger*.

- Banks don't just loan money; they assure a community has capital to build schools and critical infrastructure to bring jobs to the area. A purpose-focused bank might be a paternal advocate for city growth dedicated to making **great jobs available to struggling families**.

- Landscaping businesses don't just cut grass and trim hedges. Well-manicured neighborhoods are less likely to experience crime. A purpose-focused landscaper might be dedicated to **reducing property crime** and giving her customers the **peace of mind** that comes from knowing their families and belongings are safe.

The key is to clearly identify all the **benefits** the stakeholders experience. Sit down and talk to them. Ask them to describe:

- The benefits your products deliver.

- How those benefits make them feel about **themselves**.

- What the specific consequences are of those good feelings and benefits.

- The greater good for themselves, their families, and their community that come as a result of using your products.

- How they communicate their connection to your organizational purpose.

We find that most companies are so single-mindedly focused on day-to-day operations that they rarely stop to consider the greater good they're doing in the long term. It's time your company fully appreciates the power it has and the awesome good things it does. Employees at purpose-focused companies don't just have a job, they have a **daily calling**.

The employees at REI come to work each day to share in the company's purpose to bring the joys of outdoor living to a cubicle-imprisoned nation. The companies who supply Whole Foods Markets don't just restock the bulk food bins, they are helping to teach a nutrient-starved world how to live longer and healthier by eating right.

BEGINNING THE FORMAL INTERNAL ASSESSMENT PROCESS

After you have had a lot of conversations about purpose with your coworkers, it's time to start approaching the managers of the company. Consider recruiting a few fellow employees to join you. Approach the conversation with a spirit of learning more. Just as you did with your coworkers, ask for clarification on how the managers envision the company's purpose. Share your thoughts. Carefully ponder the manager's ideas and look for common ground.

The next step in this process is to work with management to organize formal listening sessions with all the employees in the company. Work with your managers to arrange for small teams to get together and discuss their vision for the company's purpose. Assign each group the task of creating a short written report that outlines *all* the ideas presented in their meeting. Include everything, even the implausible and crazy purposes.

We recommend that the group assignments *not* be organized by department. Try bringing together different team members from different departments. This helps the groups build consensus that reflect the needs of the entire company, not just the requirements of a particular work specialty. This also will help build staff cohesion. When a salesperson hears the business purpose ideas of someone in operations, it can be quite enlightening and vice versa.

The benefit of these small group discussions is twofold. We want to hear the best ideas from everyone in the company, but an equally powerful effect is that everyone gets a chance to be heard. If you are to implement your purpose effectively, everyone needs to know they had a hand in its formulation. You need the input of the people closest to your customers and suppliers—the frontline employees.

After completing the small group meetings, gather together all of the reports and publish the entire list of possible purposes to everyone in the company. Categorize them by type. Some might be about improving family life. Others might be about helping the environment. Let everyone read every idea. Encourage the staff to talk among themselves and have further discussions.

ASSESSING THE CHALLENGES AND OBSTACLES

Next, it's time to get real about what's actually possible. Assemble the management team and methodically list the economic, cultural, and competitive realities that will influence the choice of purpose.

Start with financial realities. Are budget cuts coming? List that. Is a competitor eroding market share? List that. Are you willing to invest in specific areas right now? List those. Catalog all your economic hurdles and opportunities.

Next, what will your company culture embrace? Is there an intrinsic sense of purpose shared by your team already? Flesh that out. Is there a bold in-house or corporate leader with a burning passion in her heart? Are there small groups within the company that have already established a departmental purpose? See if that purpose might be a match for a purpose for the whole company.

While it is important to acknowledge and embrace the positive aspects of your company culture, it is equally important to acknowledge the foibles, dysfunctions, and limitations of your team. Are they scared to try new things? Acknowledge that. Is there labor unrest? Own that. Is your team exhausted from fighting off a recent competitive threat? Inventory all of the eccentricities of your team and write those out.

Don't kid yourself here. Too many of the purpose statements we've encountered in our training and consulting work turn out be optimistic dreams with unattainable goals. The successful ones have refreshingly pragmatic goals that are actually attainable. The best plans are ambitious but are careful never to overreach. Don't dwell on negative attributes to the point of pessimism, but be very clear on what's plausible and what's not. Better a smaller purpose you accomplish than a lofty one that is quickly discarded.

HONOR YOUR COMPANY CULTURE

We find that the plans that work best are the ones where the company simply focuses on and hones what has always existed within the company culture. A lot of people in any business tend to share a similar outlook on their work and its value for shareholders. It is a far easier job to interpret and clarify existing beliefs than to start something new. Once you thoroughly understand the essential foundational beliefs of the team, you can simply uncover what has always existed and continue the journey.

It is often a good idea to look for your purpose within the projects and priorities that continually get the most attention. Seek to attach your company's purpose to the things that already have excitement and momentum within your company.

Where is the buzz and enthusiasm within the walls of your company? Is there a corporate initiative that is well-established and well-funded? Is there a thorny problem that everyone in the company is excited to undertake? Be sure to pick something with staying power. Remember, if you pick wisely, your purpose can be a guiding force for decades.

NARROWING THE POSSIBILITIES

After the management team has evaluated each purpose idea proposed by the staff, it's time to report back to the team on the ones that managers feel fit the company best. Give feedback on each of the main purposes the staff suggested. We recommend you use the following format:

- **Purposes that are possibilities**

  Explain why you like them and why you think they are a good fit for the company.

- **Purposes that are not possible**

Typically, these are purposes that have logistical reasons for rejection. They might be too expensive. They might not mesh with the company's sales strategy. Necessary resources might not be available. Thoroughly explain the reasons behind the rejection of each of these purposes.

- **Purposes that are possible but would be very difficult**

  List the pros and cons of each purpose. Clearly point out what would be required if these purposes were implemented.

- **Purposes that are possible but require more study**

  Lay out the questions that need to be answered. Report on what's being done and when you will report back to the team with additional findings.

GET MORE FEEDBACK FROM THE STAFF

After you have finished your research on the last category in the paragraph above, it's time to get more feedback from the staff. Publish a list of the purpose finalists and get staff feedback from each department. Look for honest feedback on how well each purpose would work within the daily operations of each department. Query sales, operations, marketing, and every department in the building. Encourage them to be brutally honest about the viability of each one.

The goal here is to find out if the purposes you've picked can actually be implemented. Are the purpose finalists just an abstract concept? Which ones can actually mesh well with your existing system? How exactly would the purpose show up each day? How would each department change its workflow to make the purpose a reality?

Be very firm with yourself at this stage. Most people in the business world have been through painfully self-indulgent corporate vision exercises in the past. You will most likely encounter some healthy skepticism. Encourage the team to thoroughly vet each purpose. Ask them to explore the practicality of each finalist and come up with a list of how each could mesh with existing company priorities.

After you've assessed the staff feedback, you'll have four possible options:

1. There is consensus on a single finalist.
2. There is strong support for more than one finalist.
3. There is lukewarm support for one or more finalists.
4. There is little support for any of the finalists.

If you're in the first two categories and have found one or more purposes that fit, congratulations! You're ready to move on to the next steps.

If you're in the latter two categories and found little or no support for your list of possible business purposes, you've still got work ahead of you. Many businesses find themselves at this disappointing crossroad. They have put a lot of hard work into listening and a crafting purpose statement. When their ideas are greeted with an indifferent yawn or even condescension, it can be disheartening. However, this isn't a failure. It's a sign that more investigation is required.

We find that these are the most common reasons businesses have difficulty finding their purpose:

THE PURPOSES BEING CONSIDERED ARE TOO LOFTY

The best purposes live side by side with the day-to-day operations of the business. Overly altruistic purposes tend to be abstract and need to be recrafted so they can coexist with the very real problems the team faces each day. Maybe you need to dial back your expectations. Instead of saving the whole planet, start by helping one constituency that is vital in your business's daily operations.

MANAGEMENT NEEDS TO LISTEN HARDER

The workflow of this entire process has been designed to be bottom up, not top down. If all the listening and discussion with the team did not find consensus, it could mean that something got lost in translation when the leaders honed the list of possible purposes.

We find that in some situations, the staff articulates their preferences and the managers simply don't like what they hear. The staff's purpose preferences may be far removed from the business's sales and operations goals. The purpose may directly contrast with the path that leadership has set for the company.

The good news is that we find that common ground can usually be found. It simply requires the management team to roll up their sleeves and get more imaginative on ways that business goals and purpose can get along. It may also require management to revise its business goals. If the priority business goals directly conflict with the staff's perceived purpose of itself, those goals will not be successful in the long run. Very few people come to work in the morning with a fire in their belly to hit the Wall Street estimates for the upcoming quarter.

The best companies find their business goals by clearly understanding the priorities of the staff and then finding a balance. Smart leaders clearly grasp the motivations behind the hopes and dreams of their team. Those leaders then carefully grow sales and operations goals in the fertile soil of the authentic motivations of the people who work with them.

MORE SERIOUS PROBLEMS NEED TO BE ADDRESSED FIRST

The premise of Maslow's Hiergraphy of Needs theory is that basic needs can preclude consideration of higher, more contemplative needs. If you are starving, finding a purpose for your life will probably never enter your mind. The same is true for businesses.

Unfortunately, we sometimes find that when the staff is asked to define the purpose for the business, the discussions quickly regress into a gripe session about everything that's not working on the job. There is always a little of this any time co-workers get together, but if it is pervasive, it is time to take a step back and assess.

Does your business need to take care of more fundamental survival needs that are further down the ladder on Maslow's hierarchy? People who live in constant worry of layoffs or other threats to their basic security are unfortunately in the rudimentary mindset of Maslow's physiological or safety mode. They're worried about simple survival for themselves and their families. Their focus is on paying the rent and putting food on the table.

Any talk of a progressive purpose statement will probably be greeted with inattention, skepticism or both. Their mindset of the entire purpose discussion understandably will be motivated by their own personal survival. Their response is not just an attitude; it's instinctually driven. Discussions of higher concepts like purpose will fall upon deaf ears.

Great purpose-driven companies often find themselves facing a crisis and must step back to take care of the basic needs of both the business and their team. Our research shows that purpose-driven businesses usually weather a crisis better. Just as with an army that faces adversity, shared commitment is what bonds a team.

Purpose is what gives armies their power. They didn't gather together a bunch of men and women then look for a purpose to stand for. Their nationalistic or moral conviction is the bedrock of an army's very existence. Soldiers can stick together through literal life-threatening challenges because of the strength of this conviction.

If your company is living in survival mode right now and you have not yet formulated a strong purpose, don't try and initiate it when your team is ducking for cover in foxholes. It simply won't work. Fix your immediate problems. Get things stabilized. Then try again in the future.

We see this a lot in our consulting work. A company will undergo a huge challenge like COVID-19 and things begin to fall apart. In order to save itself, the company will seek to redefine its purpose and business practices. While it is wonderful that they're ready to change to a more effective strategy, change management for a team of people running for their lives is rarely effective.

DON'T KID YOURSELF

It is important that you honestly acknowledge the emotional state of your stakeholders. We have had the heartbreaking task of working with businesses that were chomping at the bit to define their purpose, but we had to tell them to go back and fix the basics first. Finding and implementing purpose-driven business strategies is hard for even the healthiest companies. Companies experiencing ongoing crises must find a way to stop the drama. Only then can they implement a purpose-driven brand.

But don't let this stop you from thinking through what your purpose might be. There is lots of hard work that can be done right now, work that can be implemented once the basic problems are fixed. Don't wait until everything is perfect to start. Begin the discussion now as you work through operational problems. Focus your management team. Plan your discussions with staff. Identify your very best features and benefits, then come up with new ways those products could serve all your stakeholders.

IMPLEMENTATION

Once your purpose is defined, it's important that you write it down on paper so that everyone in the company can easily understand it. Great business purpose statements are one or two sentences long and easy understood by everyone. Here are some examples from other industries:

Security Company: To empower hardworking Texas families to live safer, more prosperous lives that are free from fear.

Organizational Consultant: To help Coloradans get more accomplished, reduce stress and feel more in control of their daily tasks.

Bank: To help families be ready for tough economic challenges and rise up to live more prosperous lives.

Church: To bring renewed hope into the lives of everyone in our community. We are steadfastly committed to showing how faith can bring peace to any life.

Home Builder: To facilitate families coming together by designing innovative spaces where people can interact and share in entirely new ways.

Manicurist: To be a refuge from the fast-paced demands of modern life. We will bring a new vitality to tired people and help them face the world with enthusiasm and vigor.

Lawyer: To give the people of Topeka a fair shot at competing for a better life. We will be advocates for middle-class Midwesterners in their quest for a level playing field.

What you should notice is that every one of those statements directly addresses what the company will do to empower *the lives of others and their community*. Each one deals *directly* with the change they hope to foster. They're putting a stake in the ground, declaring the transformation they will bring to the world.

A PURPOSE STATEMENT SHOULD NOT DESCRIBE THE BASIC OPERATIONS OF THE COMPANY.

Most business are proud parents and tend to feel their daily business practices are pretty awesome. Their inclination is to make the purpose statement all about *them*, not their *stakeholders*. Here are some bad examples of self-absorbed purpose statements from other industries:

- We will produce the highest quality automotive parts and provide them at a reasonable price so our customers can repair their own vehicles and save money.

- We will manufacture ski equipment that is safe, dependable and provides an optimal outdoor experience for people of all ages.

If you find your purpose statement does little more than describe what you do in a day, try fixing it by adding the following addendum to the end of the statement: "and we do this because we hope to empower our stakeholders to. . ."

So here is a self-absorbed purpose statement:

"Our sports blog will provide the people of Smithville with all the latest information about local sports teams and the standout athletes in our community. . ."

Notice how this describes the basic operation of most all sports blogs. It does not address the *effects* of that sports blog. So let's add our little addendum to this lackluster statement, then re-write a more powerful purpose statement.

First, the self-absorbed statement:

"Our sports blog will provide the people of Smithville with all the latest information about local sports teams and the standout athletes in our community . . . "

Now add the addendum:

". . . and we do this because we hope to empower our stakeholders to . . ."

Finally, write a powerful purpose statement:

". . . provide greater financial, community, and scholarship support to local sports teams and local athletes. We want to create more opportunities for kids to participate in sports and get more local kids a sports scholarship."

After going through this little exercise, we can drop the whole self-absorbed beginning. It isn't necessary because their stakeholders want to hear how they'll bring beneficial change to customer's lives and the world. They have little concern to know more about how the business operates. The powerful purpose statement at the end is all that is needed: "Our sports blog will provide greater financial, community, and scholarship support to local sports teams and local athletes and create more opportunities for kids to participate in sports and get more local kids a sports scholarship."

A PURPOSE STATEMENT SHOULD NOT DESCRIBE THE VALUES OR ETHICS OF THE BUSINESS

Formulating the beliefs that drive a business is a great exercise to undertake prior to writing a purpose statement. Articulating the ethical principles that will be the moral compass of the organization helps create a more grounded purpose.

We find ethical principles are particularly valuable in guiding a business through adversity. Clearly defining the ethical boundaries of the business can keep companies from straying into trouble when the temptation to regress is greatest.

Unfortunately, we find that most business's ethical documents tend to be more of a public relations tool than an actual operational guide. Typically the ethical bar is set quite low. These documents tend to espouse the baseline values for being a functioning member of society. For example: don't lie, no physical violence, be a team player, respect others, etc.

Wal-Mart has a whopping 11 guiding principles. What employee could recall 11 things, let alone live by them? Here are the first four principles:

1. Always act with integrity.

2. Lead with integrity, and expect others to work with integrity.

3. Follow the law at all times.

4. Be honest and fair.

What you will notice is that this is the same basic "integrity" principle stated four different ways. If a company needs to reiterate an ethical code of conduct that bans only reprehensible behavior, the business probably has much bigger problems. The rule we like to follow is that if the ethical standards listed in the document were taught in kindergarten, that's probably a sign that the code of ethics needs to evolve.

Ethics and values documents have their place, but they are not a replacement for a strong purpose. The problem is that ethics has its foundation in **contemplation**. Purpose statements are grounded in **action** and **change**. Purpose statements are the catalyst of a mission that will move out into the world boldly and transform lives. By all means, companies should define their ethical standards, but ethical documents tend to be reference material, not a guide for metamorphosis. Purpose statements can move you forward. Unfortunately, the professorial nature of ethics documents tend to banish them to the unvisited pages of the company website.

A PURPOSE STATEMENT SHOULD NOT DESCRIBE THE ACTIONS THAT WILL BE TAKEN TO FULFILL THE PURPOSE.

The methodical workflow looks like this: ethical goals > purpose goals > tactical goals. A business purpose must be clearly articulated and properly documented prior to implementation of that purpose.

We find that after working hard on finding a purpose, businesses get very excited about its creation. They want to get going and show the world the amazing things they hope to accomplish. The temptation is to stuff the purpose statement full of the tactics the company will use to implement its powerful purpose.

These additions make the purpose long and hard to live by. Great purpose statements are short and packed with meaning. They do not delve into "how"; they are firmly focused on "why." Do your best to cut every extra word from your purpose statement and move the plans for implementation and tactics to a subsequent document.

CHAPTER 13

IMPLEMENTING YOUR PURPOSE

"But with lots of good ideas, implementation is the key,
and so we need to keep our eye on the ball as
we go forward."

— Mitchell Reiss

Once your purpose statement is written, it's time to turn that statement into an action plan. The great news is that there are probably many companies and people who have similar purposes to your own.

You're about to start making some new friends. Typically, we find them to be a fascinating group. Anyone who has the drive and initiative to go through the purpose formation process is probably someone pretty special. They are innovators who want to reinvent themselves, their companies, and the world in exciting new ways. They are usually very big thinkers with kind hearts.

COMPETITIVE ASSESSMENT

Reacquaint yourself with the brand positions and mission statements of your competitors. Hopefully your purpose statement differentiates you from your major competitors, but if you find it's a close match, you'll need to make sure your tactics create a strong separation. Seek to set yourself apart. Resist the temptation to play follow the leader. If your competitor has done it, you must either do it amazingly better or choose another way to demonstrate your purpose.

INDUSTRY ASSESSMENT

Next, make your scope wider. Hop on the internet and start searching for other companies in promotional products with strong purpose statements. Below are key phrases you might want to use:

- Mission statement
- Purpose statement
- Ethics statement
- Vision statement
- Values statement
- Sustainability statement

Objectives

Expect to see a lot of mediocrity as you embark on this inventory of other organizations in the industry. Most of these statements will be little more than a description of basic business practices and unimplemented dreams of a perfect world. Stick with it. There's some good stuff out there if you do some digging.

GET OUTSIDE YOUR INDUSTRY

Your greatest teachers probably don't reside within the safe confines of promotional products; they are out there in completely different professions. The goal here is to shake off conventional thinking and pick the brains of people who share your purpose. You'll be amazed what you find outside your own sandbox. You can then adapt the good ideas so they fit in your business model.

A wonderful attribute of purpose statements is that they tend to cross sector borders splendidly. For example, your business purpose might be to empower mothers to spend more time with their children. There are amazing numbers of companies around the world who share this goal. Appleby's takeout wants Mom to spend less time cooking and more time with her family. The website elearningforkids.com wants the kids to get through homework faster. Ford wants to build cars that foster family sharing during the daily commute.

Start by weaning yourself from the need to compulsively track your major competitors. Most managers are intimately familiar with every twist and turn made by their rivals. They can describe every scheme and strategy being implemented. Businesses can often overreact. Staying abreast of competitive trends is a sound basic business strategy, but many take this too far. If a major rival makes a move, there is often a knee-jerk reaction. This gives the staff whiplash and distracts from the primary goals of the company.

Your best ideas on implementing your purpose will probably come from companies unfettered by the confines of the conventional thinking common to promotional products. We all spend most of our days inside our own industry-specific walled garden. It's comfortable there, but the steadiness of our routine makes it hard to imagine differently. There might be a local restaurant or a bank in your community that shares your same purpose. They may have already made some amazing inroads that could be a powerful lesson for you.

For example, let's say your purpose is to make local communities safer. What other companies share this mission? There is much you could learn about purpose implementation from companies such as Volvo, Schwab Investments, Tylenol, Michelin Tires, Nationwide Insurance, and the CDC. All these companies are dedicated to making people feel safe. What was their breakthrough messaging? What's on their social feed? What events and programs have they implemented?

Carefully study the customer interactions of these businesses. We find that purpose-driven businesses tend to be more committed to their customers' well-being. So many businesses limit their interact with a customer to when she's purchasing the product. They don't really see her as a flesh-and-blood person; they see her as a sale to be made. Their interaction and concern for her begins and ends with her purchase behavior. If she suddenly stops buying, she's dead to the company.

RECRUIT YOUR SHARED-PURPOSE TRIBE

One of the toughest aspects of following the traditional business model is that it can be a tremendously isolating journey. You have the camaraderie of coworkers, but if the company's goal is solely its own prosperity, those outside the business don't usually show a lot of interest. When a company's goals are inwardly obsessed, they often will compartmentalize interactions with the world. Those outside the company are classified in one of three categories: competitors, prospects, or distractions. The team hunkers down and prepares to do battle with the forces that will keep them from reaching their internal goals.

If the team's inspiration is solely limited to monthly sales goals or operational benchmarks, it's tough to find the motivation to go to work some days. Few people wake up in the morning with a smile on their face dreaming about the joy of achieving this month's benchmarks.

Purpose-driven businesses are different. When a company stands up and declares its authentic purpose to the world, like-minded people and businesses tend to suddenly appear from out of nowhere. They are often hungry for collaboration.

This collaboration is one of the most powerful benefits of declaring a strong company purpose. When the focus of a business expands to include providing the greater good for a wider group of stakeholders, those stakeholders will often step up, offering up their own unique skills and expertise. When the goal is bigger than just your own bottom line, others take notice. That goal also helps to demonstrate authenticity, which builds trust. And when trust flourishes, cooperation blooms.

Now is the time that you should reach out to other businesses and people who share your purpose. The goal is to create a cross-discipline, cross-industry group who all share a passion for your common purpose. These people will be your support group, your sounding board, and most importantly, your collaborators.

START LOCAL

Are there suppliers, vendors, or other current business partners who might be interested in joining you? Companies that do business with your company often share a similar customer base. If these company partners have not formally declared their business purpose, they might be interested in adopting yours.

Pay particular attention to companies that have similar clientele to your own. Put the word out through local business associations such as the Chamber of Commerce, the Better Business Bureau, professional associations and cause-related groups within the area. Get in touch with local politicians to ask their advice in finding like-minded business contacts. Politicians are usually amazingly well connected with other businesses in the area and are often willing to provide an introduction.

TAP YOUR TEAM'S CONTACT LIST

Plumb the contact list of your coworkers and colleagues. Put the word out to your team that you are looking for businesses and people who share your purpose.

Reach out on all your social networks. Let the world know your company's purpose then solicit your network to help find other like-minded companies and individuals.

Search specific keywords associated with your purpose and refine your searches geographically. LinkedIn provides great search tools that allow you to do very refined searches by locality, sector, interests, and keywords. If you do not have a pro-level LinkedIn account or have few LinkedIn contacts, search out a more well-connect colleague to do the search for you.

Team up with other colleagues at work to amplify your social exposure through synchronized posting and events. Solicit followers of your purpose to join in utilizing planned social events such as Twitter thunderclaps. A social message with a purpose is powerfully appealing, so be sure you lead boldly with your goal to improve the lives of your stakeholders. The smart use of promotional marketing items that align with your new purpose statement are clear reminders to employees, clients, and prospects alike of the ways your brand communicates its alignment with company purpose. A company with a stated intent to support causes for veterans would be well-suited to outfit their staff with BASECAMP backpacks that support Wounded Warrior Project.

SET UP ONGOING SYSTEMS FOR SHARING

Once you have solicited your network, build systems to make sure you stay connected. Social sharing tools are your best bet. Create purpose-driven groups on LinkedIn and Facebook. This is a place where you can post problems and get help from others in achieving your goals.

Finally, send specific invitations to a select few individuals in the group to form a mastermind group. This is a small group of no more than ten people. Recruit the very best minds, the most capable achievers, and the power brokers. These will be your big-brain advisors who all help one another achieve their shared purpose. Geography should be no obstacle. Seek out the very best people in the world.

We recommend that the mastermind group meet using video conferencing services such as Webex, Skype, or Zoom. There is something magical about seeing people face-to-face, and a group this size will be able to have wonderfully personal discussions using video.

SET UP STAKEHOLDER FEEDBACK SYSTEMS

You cannot help your stakeholders without an extensive understanding of their hopes, challenges, and problems. Before you launch into empowering new options for them, you will want to get a lot of feedback from the people who will be on the receiving end of your work. You will eliminate *a lot* of heartache, wasted time, and wasted money if you simply sit down with them and ask them to describe the things about their lives they hope to change.

We usually do this in small groups of fewer than ten people. Buy a few pizzas and gather your stakeholders together for an informal feedback session. Try not to do it at your place of business. Instead, choose more neutral ground like a local library, community hall, coffee shop, or some other place conducive to conversation.

Remember that you are there to talk about *them*, not you. Do not ask them "how do you like my product." Your products probably generate scant attention in their lives. Your stakeholders probably rarely think much about your promotional products.

Their mental attention is dominated by the really important things they hope to achieve in their careers, for their families, and in their personal life. These are the things vital to their happiness, and it's your job to understand how these vitally important motivators drive their attitudes and behaviors. Once you understand these motivations, it's your job to mold the features of your products, operations, and company purpose to serve these important needs. By aligning the products you source with your purpose, you're able to extend your brand story in ways your competition can't comprehend. By supporting causes your team is passionate about, you offer your prospects, client, and employees an opportunity to gravitate to you out of shared passion instead of dollars and cents alone.

CHAPTER 14

BUILDING THE ACTION PLAN

"Have a bias toward action - let's see something happen now. You can break that big plan into small steps and take the first step right away."

— Indira Gandhi

There are limitless ways to implement your purpose. Your company will need to find the way that best fits your company culture, competitive situation, and timeline. Here are some things to keep in mind and some characteristics of companies that have been successful.

BUILD AND INTEGRATE YOUR PURPOSE TACTICS

It is easy to get caught up in the altruistic high that comes from planning the good your company wants to do in the world. We find that some companies tend to get swept up in the euphoria. They plan *big* with hopes of having a real impact. It is good to put together a plan with some meat to it, but if that plan detracts from the efficient day-to-day operations of the business, it serves no one.

Your purpose has two very critical jobs to accomplish. It must uplift your stakeholders *AND* it must make lots of money. If your purpose does only the first of these tasks, neither the purpose nor the company will survive. You must build a purpose that pleases both the heart-line and the bottom-line.

The best way to assure a profitable purpose is to tightly integrate it with the frontline products and business practices that generate the most cash inside your company. Purposes that neglect this have a tendency to quickly become irrelevant because they are not a vital part of the business cash flow. A purpose that is a foundational element of your most important daily operations is one that tends to get implemented.

Use your own best business practices as your anchor and look for ways those workflows can be modified to encompass your purpose. It is exciting to launch a purpose and state your goals, but it is even more important that your purpose settles into a delightfully habitual routine. The best purposes are day in, day out, accomplished in a thousand small ways. Seek methodical integration in every place your company touches a stakeholder.

For example, the sales team at Patagonia is constantly building websites, pitch proposals, and social media posts that discuss sustainability. Their engineering teams are constantly innovating new materials, new supply chains, and new testing procedures that push the boundaries of sustainable manufacturing. Patagonia's purpose of sustainability is not hard to integrate because the company has made it the centerpiece of all their marketing, sales, and operations strategies. From how they take out their trash to how they develop new products to how they compensate their CEO, Patagonia's purpose is the baseline of the entire business plan.

INTEGRATE PURPOSE WITH PRIORITIES

Get incredibly granular on how purpose will show up each day. Follow the internal trail your stakeholders use to interact with your company. Look for small opportunities all along the way. What is said on the phone when potential customers call your business? How does purpose show up on your website on the very first page? How is purpose demonstrated on a service call? How is purpose proven when customers complain?

When your team develops the proposals and builds the products by continually coming back to the words of your purpose, the sheer repetition builds familiarity and makes it a habit. The best purpose driven plans are the ones implemented in hundreds of small ways in hundreds of small places all across the business day. Little things can truly make the biggest difference.

MAKE MANAGEMENT THE DRIVING FORCE

Too often we have seen companies create amazing purposes that are quickly delegated to committees, HR, or other peripheral groups within the company. Building a purpose-driven company is an incredibly hard change. If you hope to keep it alive, someone with real power within the organization must be its champion. Hopefully that will be the entire senior management team.

SET UP ACCOUNTABILITY SYSTEMS

Don't just create a plan "to do better." Give yourself specific landmarks and benchmarks and set hard dates to get them done. Make sure the programs have the necessary resources and personnel behind them to achieve them.

SHOW YOUR TEAM: NOT ANOTHER DOOMED PLAN

After the plan is launched, plan a major event to demonstrate that the company is serious about making purpose a part of its business operations. Remember, most employees have seen a myriad of CSR plans come and go. Too many staffers have learned just to play along and hope that management loses interest. Roll out your plan with some real fanfare and a carefully considered internal communication strategy. Promotional marketing consultants would URGE you to include items branded with messaging to reinforce your commitment to your new CSR strategy. Products from our marketplace have ties to almost any CSR objective conceivable, and many programs allow you to request an outcome specific to the non-profit of your choice. These options expand monthly, as more partners in our marketplace realize the value of these programs and develop their own.

Be sure to follow up with regular progress reports to your team. The most authentic demonstration of your commitment is persistence. Keep the conversation going day after day, month after month. Don't just share the victories; keep your team abreast of the setbacks as well, including what is being done to move forward.

PURPOSE IS MORE THAN MARKETING

Talk is cheap and marketing talk is the cheapest of all. Companies often have a tendency to crank up the purpose-driven marketing messaging, then hope the product lines and operations will catch up later. Mistrust of marketing is endemic. Advertising can point out how a great purpose is implemented, but it can't be a replacement for palpable proof that the company is walking its talk. If you or your clients fake it, your stakeholders will call you out, exposing the ugly truth all over social media. Make sure front-line customer experience provides substantive evidence of genuine commitment.

AVOID OVERREACHING

It is far better to start with modest, yet attainable goals than it is to create big plans that fail and leave your team disheartened. Plan for a lot of incremental wins. This will eventually lead to exponential success and a steady routine of purpose-driven victories. The more your teams see your purpose in action, the more they will know you're serious.

AVOID UNDER REACHING

After doing all the hard work of finding your purpose and creating a plan, the temptation is to let your hair down a bit and relax after the plan has been written. Starting is always the toughest part so you need to make sure you kick this thing off right. Clearly lay out your expectations on new ways of doing business. Plan regular check-ins and progress reports.

SHARE YOUR NEW BENCHMARKS WITH STAKEHOLDERS

If you really want to assure steady progress on your purpose-driven path, then blow up the bridges behind you. Create a system that does not allow retreat and backtracking. The best way to accomplish this is to very *publicly* declare your mission and the goals you will achieve. Throw it out to the whole world. Give them dates it will be done. Give them landmarks you will reach. The threat of a very public humiliation will keep you and your entire team on track to get it done.

RECRUIT AN ADVISORY GROUP

Gather together a group of your most capable purpose-driven leaders from outside the company. Task them with two jobs: first, to advise you on the best ways to move forward. Second, to provide continual feedback on the effectiveness of your purpose-driven implementation. Outside people not invested in the internal politics of your company will provide invaluable feedback on where you are excelling and where you need work.

MAKING PURPOSE PART OF YOUR DAILY WORKFLOW

Identifying and implementing a powerful business purpose isn't just a professional endeavor; it often spills over into our personal lives as well. After working this hard to identify a transcendent company mission, it's only natural to start asking questions about how purpose plays a role in our individual lives.

The path of purpose-driven business leadership is an arduous one, but we are continually inspired and amazed that so many people turn this professional journey into a catalyst for deep changes in other parts of their life.

It's only natural to seek meaning in our careers. Most of us feel our job is one of the most powerful shapers of our destiny. The majority of people we have worked with in our careers enthusiastically do more than is required on the job. They are often most enrolled in their lives when a job challenges them to rise up and tackle an important business obstacle. Most of them put their very hearts and souls into their jobs. They feel deep affection, even love, for many of their coworkers. They beam with pride when their team rallies to achieve a difficult goal.

Our careers shape our destiny in so many ways. All of us have many roles in life: parent, brother/sister, spouse, mentor, friend. But when someone asks us what we do, most of us reflexively describe our professional life. Many of us have left high-paying but soulless jobs in exchange for lower paying, more meaningful work. Today's leaner economic times mean a lot of us spend more time interacting with our coworkers than with our families.

Fully embracing a business purpose brings an entirely new storyline to our own very personal daily toil. This purpose is inherent in some professions. Nurses can go to work each day knowing they are saving lives. Teachers know they are molding the destiny of the next generation. Architects build spaces that shape how communities grow.

But most of us work in jobs where the bigger purpose can be more difficult to see. On that cold morning after a long weekend, it's hard to identify how answering those 50 neglected emails can help make the world a better place. It's difficult to find meaning in yet another conference call with the regional manager.

It's easy to fixate on the drudgery inherent in any job. The escape from this self-destructive loop is continually reconnecting with your business purpose. When times are most frustrating, this simple practice can shift your entire mindset. But it requires an unceasing discipline to climb out of the daily-grind attitude. You must recognize and fully appreciate the difference your business makes in the lives of stakeholders.

That bank teller is not just counting money in his change drawer. He is part of a team that's helping local families afford college for his kids. He can perceive that next person in the bank line as just another faceless soul who needs a check cashed, or he can see that person as another parent he's empowering to achieve a family mission.

Maintaining this larger view is often easier in our personal lives. We feel good when we sacrifice to help a friend. We perceive driving our kids to soccer practice as more fun than driving to work. It feels pretty nice to slide the envelope into the church collection plate. Why? Because we get an opportunity to reconnect with a bigger, more meaningful mission.

We perceive the lack of a raise at work as a major injustice yet we gladly put up with less money to spend on lunch to pay for an expensive prom dress for our daughter. The net effect is the same. Both scenarios leave us with less money. The difference is we resent losing money when we are out of touch with the purpose of our work. Lack of a raise will seem a lot more endurable when we have the confidence that our work is empowering others.

It is vitally important that you fully step into the wisdom that your job is doing powerful good in the world every day. Your task is to do a better job of **noticing that good**. If you want to feel more fulfilled in your career and enjoy your workday more, make your company's business purpose the centerpiece of your own daily work routine. Build reminders into your day. Put it at the top of your to-do list. Put the words in a frame on the wall. Put it on a Post-It note in your car. Say an affirmation every time you walk through the front door. Not many people spend their own money to buy items with their company logo, but really top-notch branded merchandise from your company that supports the non-profit you care about might change your mind.

Redefine your own personal job title. When people ask you what you do, don't describe your position, describe your business purpose. Your work colleagues may call you a sales rep, but you know you are really a grower of B2B organizations.

Be a catalyst to enroll others in your company. Bring it up in meetings. Mention it at the water cooler. Celebrate when your purpose pays off with your stakeholders. The more you **personally** spread the word, the better you will feel about why you come to work. Be a purpose evangelist.

The most powerful force in the world is not government, religion, or culture. It's business. If you want to leave a powerful legacy in this life, begin by changing the way you do business.

CHAPTER 15

THE R.U.L.E.S.

"Constancy to purpose is the secret of success."

— Benjamin Disraeli

There are R.U.L.E.S. to be mindful of when bringing your purpose to life. Here are 10 questions to ask as you create your Red Goldfish:

R – RESONATE

- Will this connect with both employees and customers?

- Is it something that is meaningful to the purpose of your brand?

U – UNIQUE

- Will this stand out in the marketplace?

- Can you avoid being seen as "me to" or generic?

L – LEGITIMATE

- Is the Red Goldfish making a sufficient impact?

- Will it be seen as authentic when connected to the purpose of your brand?

E – EMOTIONAL

- Will this make an emotional connection with your stakeholders?

- Does it strike an emotional chord and will people care about your effort?

S - STICKY

- Will it be remark-able enough to get people talking?

- Is it easily shareable?

FINAL THOUGHTS

CHAPTER 16

FIVE TOP TAKEAWAYS

"Advice is like a tablet of aspirin. It tends to work only if you take it."

— David Murphy

Here are the top five takeaways from *Red Goldfish Promo Edition*:

1. THE POWER OF AND

This is not a decision of OR. You don't need to choose profit OR purpose. You can opt for both through the power of AND by becoming a for-purpose business.

2. A NEW BULLSEYE

The new view of business places purpose first. It sits at the center of the business and informs every decision going forward.

3. THE BLURRING OF LINES

No longer will corporate filing status determine a business. The new mold is hybrid. Going forward, you will either be seen as for-purpose or not-for-purpose. Be for-purpose and be willing to tie your brand to that purpose in visible ways.

4. RISING EXPECTATIONS

Consumers and employees want to connect with a purpose beyond profit. The new expectation is that business can be a force for good. You'll need to consistently and repeatedly show your efforts toward being that force for good.

5. BIG DOORS SWING ON LITTLE HINGES

Big ideas like purpose need to be lived every day. Beyond words, it's the little things that bring the purpose to life. These Red Goldfish are the straws that stir the drink.

ABOUT THE AUTHORS

STAN PHELPS

Stan Phelps is a best-selling author, keynote speaker, and workshop facilitator. He believes that today's organizations must focus on meaningful differentiation to win the hearts of both employees and customers.

He is the founder of PurpleGoldfish.com. Purple Goldfish is a think tank of customer experience and employee engagement experts that offers keynotes and workshops that drive loyalty and sales. The group helps organizations connect with the hearts and minds of customers and employees.

Prior to PurpleGoldfish.com, Stan had a 20-year career in marketing that included leadership positions at IMG, adidas, PGA Exhibitions, and Synergy. At Synergy, he worked on award-winning experiential programs for top brands such as KFC, Wachovia, NASCAR, Starbucks, and M&M's.

Stan is a TEDx speaker, a Forbes contributor, and an IBM Futurist. His writing is syndicated on top sites such as Customer Think and Business2Community. He has spoken at more than 400 events across Australia, Bahrain, Canada, Ecuador, France, Germany, Holland, Israel, Japan, Malaysia, Peru, Russia, Singapore, Spain, Sweden, UK, and the US.

He is the author of the Goldfish Series of business books:

- *Purple Goldfish 2.0 - 10 Ways to Attract Raving Customers*
- *Green Goldfish 2.0 - 15 Keys to Driving Employee Engagement*

- *Golden Goldfish - The Vital Few*

- *Blue Goldfish - Using Technology, Data, and Analytics to Drive Both Profits and Prophets*

- *Purple Goldfish Service Edition - 12 Ways Hotels, Restaurants, and Airlines Win the Right Customers*

- *Red Goldfish - Motivating Sales and Loyalty Through Shared Passion and Purpose*

- *Pink Goldfish - Defy Normal, Exploit Imperfection, and Captivate Your Customers*

- *Purple Goldfish Franchise Edition - The Ultimate S.Y.S.T.E.M. for Franchisors and Franchisees*

- *Yellow Goldfish - Nine Ways to Drive Happiness in Business for Growth, Productivity, and Prosperity*

- *Gray Goldfish - Navigating the Gray Areas to Successfully Lead Every Generation*

- *Red Goldfish Nonprofit Edition - How the Best Nonprofits Leverage Their Purpose to Increase Engagement and Impact*

- *Diamond Goldfish - Excel Under Pressure & Thrive in the Game of Business*

- *Silver Goldfish - Loud & Clear: The 10 Keys to Delivering Memorable Business Presentations*

and one fun one . . .

- *Bar Tricks, Bad Jokes, & Even Worse Stories*

Stan received a BS in Marketing and Human Resources from Marist College, a JD/MBA from Villanova University, and a certificate for Achieving Breakthrough Service from Harvard Business School. He is a Certified Net Promoter Associate, an Instructor at the ANA School of Marketing, and has taught as an adjunct professor at NYU, Rutgers University, and Manhattan-ville College.

Stan is also a fellow at Maddock Douglas, an innovation consulting firm in Chicago. Stan lives in Cary, North Carolina, with his wife, Jennifer, and their two boys, Thomas and James.

To book Stan for an upcoming keynote, webinar, virtual talk, or workshop go to stanphelpsspeaks.com. You can reach Stan at stan@purplegoldfish.com, call +1.919.360.4702, or follow him on Twitter: @StanPhelpsPG.

ROGER BURNETT

In a sales career spanning 25+ years, Roger Burnett has studied competitive differentiation and organizational behavior of top performing sales operations. His efforts to differentiate using purpose as the foundational pillar of a personal sales strategy have created noteworthy results:

- Michigan Promotional Professionals Association Board of Directors President 2011 & 2019

- Promotional Products Association International Regional Association Council Board of Directors President 2013

- Co-founder, PromoKitchen 2011 (Mentorship Chair 2013 – 2015)

- Co-founder, PromoCares 2018 (Host, PromoCares Radio podcast 2018 – 2019, executive producer 2018 – present)

- Host, So, You're in Sales? podcast (2017 – present)

- Promotional Products Association International Regional Association Council Volunteer of the Year 2018

- Monthly Blog at PromoJournal – The Burn

- Fellow – Promotional Products Association International

As founder of the social marketing agency Social Good Promotions, Roger employs a give-first strategy in developing relationships and employs a business model founded on making the world a better place and using the efforts of its employees to achieve that objective.

Roger is husband to Melisa, father to Ryan, Dylan, and Buck and a lifelong Detroit-area native. You will most often find him outside engaged in activity that includes movement and shared experiences with friends, be it boating, golfing, camping, hiking, or at a concert.

To book Roger as a speaker or facilitator for upcoming events please email roger@socialgoodpromotions.com, call 810-986-5369, or tweet @rogerburnett.

OTHER COLORS IN THE GOLDFISH SERIES

PURPLE GOLDFISH 2.0 – 10 WAYS TO ATTRACT RAVING CUSTOMERS

Purple Goldfish is based on the Purple Goldfish Project, a crowd-sourcing effort that collected more than 1,001 examples of signature-added value. The book draws inspiration from the concept of lagniappe, providing 10 practical strategies for winning the hearts of customers and influencing positive word of mouth.

GREEN GOLDFISH 2.0 – 15 KEYS TO DRIVING EMPLOYEE ENGAGEMENT

Green Goldfish is based on the simple premise that "happy engaged employees create happy enthused customers." The book focuses on 15 different ways to drive employee engagement and reinforce a strong corporate culture.

GOLDEN GOLDFISH – THE VITAL FEW

Golden Goldfish examines the importance of your top 20 percent of customers and employees. The book showcases nine ways to drive loyalty and retention with these two critical groups.

BLUE GOLDFISH - USING TECHNOLOGY, DATA, AND ANA-LYTICS TO DRIVE BOTH PROFITS AND PROPHET

Blue Goldfish examines how to leverage technology, data, and ana-lytics to do a "little something extra" to improve the experience for the customer. The book is based on a collection of over 300 case studies. It examines the three R's: Relationship, Responsiveness, and Readiness. *Blue Goldfish* uncovers eight different ways to turn insights into action.

RED GOLDFISH - MOTIVATING SALES AND LOYALTY THROUGH SHARED PASSION AND PURPOSE

Purpose is changing the way we work and how customers choose business partners. It is driving loyalty, and it's on its way to becoming the ultimate differentiator in business. *Red Goldfish* shares cutting edge examples and reveals the eight ways businesses can embrace purpose that drives employee engagement, fuels the bottom line, and makes an impact on the lives of those it serves.

PURPLE GOLDFISH SERVICE EDITION - 12 WAYS HOTELS, RESTAURANTS, AND AIRLINES WIN THE RIGHT CUSTOMERS

Purple Goldfish Service Edition is about differentiation via added value, and marketing to your existing customers via G.L.U.E. (giving little unexpected extras). Packed with over 100 examples, the book focuses on the 12 ways to do the "little extras" to improve the customer experience for restaurants, hotels, and airlines. The end result is increased sales, happier customers, and positive word of mouth.

PINK GOLDFISH - DEFY NORMAL, EXPLOIT IMPERFECTION, AND CAPTIVATE YOUR CUSTOMERS

Companies need to stand out in a crowded marketplace, but true differentiation is increasingly rare. Based on over 200 case studies, *Pink Goldfish* provides an unconventional seven-part framework for achieving competitive separation by embracing flaws instead of fixing them.

PURPLE GOLDFISH FRANCHISE EDITION - THE ULTIMATE S.Y.S.T.E.M. FOR FRANCHISORS AND FRANCHISEES

Packed with over 100 best-practice examples, *Purple Goldfish Franchise Edition* focuses on the six keys to creating a successful franchise S.Y.S.T.E.M. and a dozen ways to create a signature customer experience.

YELLOW GOLDFISH - NINE WAYS TO DRIVE HAPPINESS IN BUSINESS FOR GROWTH, PRODUCTIVITY, AND PROSPERITY

There should only be one success metric in business and that's happiness. A Yellow Goldfish is any time a business does a little extra to contribute to the happiness of its customers, employees, or society. Based on nearly 300 case studies, *Yellow Goldfish* provides a nine-part framework for happiness-driven growth, productivity, and prosperity in business.

GRAY GOLDFISH - NAVIGATING THE GRAY AREAS TO SUCCESSFULLY LEAD EVERY GENERATION

How do you successfully lead the five generations in today's workforce? You need tools to navigate. Filled with over 100 case studies and the Generational Matrix, *Gray Goldfish* provides the definitive map for leaders to follow as they recruit, train, manage, and inspire across the generations.

RED GOLDFISH NONPROFIT EDITION -

The competition is fierce in the nonprofit world, even when competing in different spaces. This book explores the signature ways nonprofits reinforce their purpose and stand out in a crowded marketplace, whether it is an extra level of recognition for key donors, a special incentive designed to keep their best employees, or something simple like a luncheon to recognize volunteers or highest fundraisers. If you work at a nonprofit, this book will help you deliver "a little extra" to your stakeholders.

DIAMOND GOLDFISH - EXCEL UNDER PRESSURE & THRIVE IN THE GAME OF BUSINESS

Diamond Goldfish uncovers how business is a game. It's a guide for driving sales and deepening client relationships. Based on the Diamond Rule, over 150 case studies, and the science-backed framework of Market Force, the book provides perspective and tools for winning in sales and client management.

SILVER GOLDFISH – LOUD & CLEAR: THE 10 KEYS TO DELIVERING MEMORABLE BUSINESS PRESENTATIONS

How do you avoid giving the typical boring corporate presentation? You need the tools and the approach to delivering memorable presentations. Filled with 64 tips, *Silver Goldfish* provides 10 keys and a six-step approach to coming across Loud & Clear when presenting.

Made in the USA
Las Vegas, NV
16 December 2020